Pearls FROM THE Quran

LESSONS FROM

Sūrah Yūsuf

سورة يوسف

DR YASIR QADHI

KUBE PUBLISHING

Lessons from Sūrah Yūsuf

First published in England by
Kube Publishing Ltd
Markfield Conference Centre,
Ratby Lane, Markfield,
Leicestershire, LE67 9SY,
United Kingdom
Tel: +44 (0) 1530 249230
Fax: +44 (0) 1530 249656
Email: info@ kubepublishing.com
Website: www.kubepublishing.com

PEARLS FROM THE QUR'AN

3rd impression, 2023

CIP data for this book is available from the British Library.

ISBN: 978-1-84774-138-7 casebound
ISBN: 978-1-84774-137-0 paperback
ISBN: 978-1-84774-139-4 ebook

Editor: Lubaaba al-Azami
Cover Design by: Jannah Haque
Typesetting by: nqaddoura@hotmail.com
Printed by: Elma Basim, Turkey

Contents

Transliteration Table

Arabic Consonants

Initial, unexpressed medial and final: ء ’

ا	a	د	d	ض	ḍ	ك	k
ب	b	ذ	dh	ط	ṭ	ل	l
ت	t	ر	r	ظ	ẓ	م	m
ث	th	ز	z	ع	‘	ن	n
ج	j	س	s	غ	gh	هـ	h
ح	ḥ	ش	sh	ف	f	و	w
خ	kh	ص	ṣ	ق	q	ي	y

With a *shaddah*, both medial and final consonants are doubled.

Vowels, diphthongs, etc.

Short:	a	ـَ	ـِ	i	ـُ	u
Long:	ā	ـَا	ـِي	ī	ـُو	ū
Diphthongs:			ـَوْ	aw		
			ـَىْ	ay		

Foreword

All Praise is due to Allah, Who revealed the Book to His Servant to be the Only Guidance, And may prayers and salutations be upon our Prophet (ﷺ) in great abundance.

The first time the Qur'ān spoke to me, it was through Sūrah Yūsuf.

I was probably 11 years old, in the mid-1980s. Like most kids my age, I had a Qur'ān teacher who helped me with reading and memorization (at this stage, I had only memorized maybe Juz ʿAmma). I didn't understand Arabic then, and while, of course, I loved listening to my father's cassettes of Abdul Basit Abdul Samad, I hadn't read any translation of the Qur'ān. One day, in the summer break, completely bored at night, I curiously pulled out an old and tattered copy of the Qur'ān from my father's library – a translation of Abdullah Yūsuf Ali. I remember flicking through it, here and there, reading passages before losing interest and then turning to another passage (I was just a child after all!).

Then, seemingly at random – but of course, it was Allah's *qadr* – I came across the beginning of Sūrah Yūsuf.

I remember it vividly: the opening line just caught me like a hook, and I spent the next hour or so – way past my bedtime – turning page after page, reading every verse, and following up with every footnote in Abdullah Yusuf Ali's translation, until finally, I finished the sūrah. I was *riveted* with the story. At night as I lay in bed, my mind became filled with images from the sūrah: Yūsuf alone in the well, the torn shirt, him sitting in the palace on the King's throne. Thus began my journey into the Qur'ān.

Five years later, I would be memorizing the entire Qur'ān, and finishing Sūrah Yūsuf in a breeze. Around a decade after I first read it, I found myself studying at the University of Madinah. I would pick up little booklets in libraries and bookstores that went into more detail regarding this sūrah: some discussed *balāgha* (Arabic eloquence), others concentrated on the morals and benefits of this story. It was here as well that I began building my personal library: every month, when the students got their modest stipend, the first thing I did was to rush to the bookstores and splurge on a book that I might have had my eyes on for a while. Slowly, my *tafsīr* collection began to grow, and whatever I could find about this sūrah, I would buy.

In the summer of 2001, I was invited for my very first trip to England (since then, to date, I have been fortunate to travel more than a hundred times to the UK), and my hosts asked what intensive class I would be interested in teaching at Masjid al-Tawhid in Leyton. Immediately, and without a moment's hesitation, I said, "I would like to teach a detailed *tafsīr* of Sūrah Yūsuf!" Perhaps the child in me was still subconsciously imagining that story.

I spent a significant portion of that summer reading the classical *tafsīrs* and sifting through material to prepare for that course. It was the first time I taught the *tafsīr* of Sūrah Yūsuf, but it would not be the last, and I would go on to teach it half a dozen times, sometimes in various masjids of cities where I lived in over the course of the next two decades, and sometimes for some Islamic satellite channels for broadcast. (That class also happened to be the first time I taught an intensive *tafsīr* class; hence it was my first exposure to the art of teaching *tafsīr* in English.) On a personal note, soon after the cassettes of that lecture were released, I was blessed with my second child, and I named him after the prophet of this sūrah. Every time I taught the sūrah, I went back to even more references and contemplated the sūrah afresh, and every time the story continued to resonate with me.

When I was approached last year by Kube Publications to publish a *tafsīr* of this sūrah in English, it was the next logical step, and I eagerly took on this task.

Tafsīr is a multidisciplinary field and one that can be done from many different angles and at numerous levels of detail. There is no 'right' or 'wrong' level, and for every style and level of detail, there is an audience that will appreciate it. To write a *tafsīr* in any language other than Arabic is a compounded dilemma: to what level should each word be dissected, and how should one explain Arabic's eloquence to a non-Arabic speaking audience?

For this work, I decided to choose a style that would be appropriate for the sūrah – easygoing and smooth, concentrating on the morals of the story rather than specific examples of Arabic eloquence. I want the reader to be immersed in the morals of the sūrah, and not get bogged down with numerous footnotes or incidental benefits that might be beneficial for advanced students but would cause others to lose track of the main point. Hence, in this book (in contrast to some of my other writings), one will not find detailed discussions of differences of opinions or competing views regarding secondary issues or references. I wanted this book to be *read*, cover to cover if possible, with the same enthusiasm as a translation of this sūrah. It is not to say that one won't find academic benefit or *tafsīr*-based points in it. On the contrary, I have consulted many works while writing this *tafsīr*, but rather than separate them into points, I have tried my utmost to incorporate their ideas into the commentary without mentioning controversies or differences.

I hope that this style combines academic benefits, spiritual motivation, and ease of reading.

The primary works that I consulted for this *tafsīr* are (in chronological order):

- *Al-Muḥarrar al-Wajīz* of Ibn ʿAṭiyya (d. 546 AH/1152 CE)
- *Zād al-Masīr* of Ibn al-Jawzī (d. 597 AH/1201 CE)
- *Tafsīr* of Ibn Kathīr (d. 774 AH/1373 CE)
- *Al-Taḥrīr wa-l-tanwīr* of Ibn ʿAshūr (d. 1973 CE)

Of course, the encyclopedic work of Ibn Jarīr al-Ṭabarī (d. 311 AH/924 CE) was always in the background, and some of the points in this work were culled from his *magnum opus*.

No work is the product of only one author. I would like to thank Sr. Shaakirah Edwards for the many hours she spent helping to smooth the rough edges and shaping the narrative-style of the work. Br. Ekram Haque gave valuable advice and feedback on an initial draft of this work. The editors of Kube also deserve special mention for their hard work and improvements. Of course, special mention must be made of my family. My three teenagers and one tween are now accustomed to leaving their father in his study for many, many hours; I hope that when they are adults, they can forgive the long absences their father had during their growing years. My wife of a quarter of a century has been my constant support and pillar, and I thank Allah for such a wonderful 'Khadījah' figure in my life. I shall always be grateful to my parents for raising me upon the foundations of this faith and instilling in me the love of the Qur'ān, and for encouraging me to memorize the Book of Allah, and then to study Islam in the city of the Prophet (ﷺ). I am fortunate that they are now living with me, and that our proximity is a source of comfort to them: *"O Allah! Have mercy on them even as they reared me as a child" [Isrā: 24].*

I pray that the readers of this book experience the same joy and enthusiasm that I felt as a child when I read this sūrah for the first time, for indeed when it comes to stories, all of us are still children!

Dr. Yasir Qadhi
Plano, TX
4th December 2020 CE
(18th Rabi' al-Thani, 1442 AH)

Introduction

Allāh called Sūrah Yūsuf the 'Best of All Stories', which He revealed in the Qur'ān, the best of all Revelations, to the best of all prophets, our Prophet Muhammad ﷺ. The story was revealed to lift his spirits at a time when his sufferings and worries had mounted. The Prophet Yūsuf lived thousands of years ago, but time has not diminished his story's relevance. It is a tale of love, passion, betrayal, and forgiveness, and it has something to teach us, at every stage of our lives. It imparts Divine wisdom wrapped in unparalleled eloquence. It is a timeless story that will continue to soothe our souls during times of hardship and reignite our trust in our Lord.

The Revelation of Sūrah Yūsuf

The timing of Sūrah Yūsuf could not be more opportune. Allāh revealed it after the 'Year of Sorrow,' in which three traumatic events happened to the Prophet ﷺ one after another.

The first was the most personal and intimate: the death of his wife, Khadījah. She was his ﷺ greatest supporter and a constant source of comfort and strength. When the revelation began, it was Khadījah that he turned to for emotional support and reassurance. She was the first to believe in his ﷺ mission and firmly remained by his side in the face of tremendous adversity. When a man has comfort and love inside his home, he can face anything in the world outside. Khadījah's death was such a profound loss for the Prophet ﷺ that he, known for his ubiquitous smile, did not smile for a whole year.

A second tragedy soon followed, the death of his uncle Abū Ṭālib. While Khadījah had been the Prophet's ﷺ supporter at home, Abū Ṭālib was his supporter in public. When the Quraysh began to threaten the Prophet ﷺ because of his public preaching, Abū Ṭālib initially tried to convince his nephew to stop. But the Prophet's response would change Abū Ṭālib's life forever. The Prophet ﷺ said, 'By Allāh! If they placed the sun in my right hand and the moon in my left on the condition that I abandon this course, I would not abandon it until Allāh has made me victorious, or I perish trying.' Abū Ṭālib then said, 'Go and preach what you please, for, by Allāh, I will never forsake you.'[1] He was a man of his word. For the next ten years, Abū Ṭālib did everything he could to protect the Prophet ﷺ. He sacrificed his reputation and prestige to protect his nephew, so much so, that when the Quraysh boycotted the Muslims, Abū Ṭālib voluntarily gave up his privileges to join them in the valley outside of Makkah. As long as Abū Ṭālib lived, the Quraysh could not harm the Prophet ﷺ. With his death,

1 *Sīrah* of Ibn Hisham (1/265).

the persecution only increased, to such an extent that the Prophet ﷺ would eventually have to leave Makkah.

The third incident was the Prophet's fateful trip to Ṭā'if to invite its people to the worship of Allāh alone. These were the most difficult days of his life. His wife 'Ā'ishah once asked him, 'Have you encountered a day harder than the Battle of Uḥud?' The Prophet ﷺ said, 'Yes. Your tribes have troubled me very much, and the worst was the day of Aqaba when I presented myself to Ibn Abd Yalīl ibn 'Amr [the chieftain of Ṭā'if], and he did not respond to what I intended. I departed, overwhelmed with excessive sorrow.'[2] The Prophet ﷺ was publicly rejected and humiliated in Ṭā'if and had stones pelted at him until his sandals filled up with blood.

These incidents occurred within six weeks of each other, and the Prophet ﷺ felt as if things couldn't get any worse. It was at this time that Allāh chose to reveal Sūrah Yūsuf. We do not know the exact date, except that it was around the tenth or eleventh year of the *da'wah* in Makkah and a few years before the *hijrah*. When we understand the time frame of revelation, the significance of Sūrah Yūsuf becomes clear. Through the revelation of Sūrah Yūsuf Allāh lifted the Prophet's spirits, and consoled and strengthened him, at a time when he was politically vulnerable. Sūrah Yūsuf was the light that brought the Prophet ﷺ out of the darkness of his pain and anguish. For centuries, before the Prophet ﷺ and since, this sūrah has uplifted the believers and illuminated their spiritual paths.

---

2 *Ṣaḥīḥ* of al-Bukhārī (3059).

The scholars have mentioned several other incidents behind the revelation of this sūrah. As the persecution of the Muslims increased, the *Ṣaḥābah* felt overwhelmed. They went to the Prophet ﷺ and said, 'O Allāh's Messenger! Why not narrate to us stories?'[3] They wanted to hear the examples of how the previous nations coped with suffering. At the same time, the Quraysh were trying to discredit the Prophet ﷺ as a messenger of God, calling him a poet, a soothsayer, and a madman. They sent a delegation to the Jews of Madīnah to ask for a question that only a prophet could answer. The Jews told them to ask about the story of Yūsuf and his brothers because they presumed that no Arab would know it. Allāh responded to their question by revealing Sūrah Yūsuf in captivating detail.

3 *Tafsīr* of al-Ṭabarī (15/552).

PART ONE

The Family of Yaʿqūb

بِسْمِ ٱللَّهِ ٱلرَّحْمَٰنِ ٱلرَّحِيمِ

In the name of Allāh, the Most Merciful, the Most Compassionate

الٓرۚ تِلْكَ ءَايَٰتُ ٱلْكِتَٰبِ ٱلْمُبِينِ ١

Alif-Lam-Ra.

These are the verses of the clear Book.

Sūrah Yūsuf begins with the letters '***Alif-Lām-Ra...***' They are called *ḥurūf al-muqaṭṭaʿāt,* or broken letters, by the scholars of *tafsīr*, because they are disjointed and do not form words. In some instances, a sūrah begins with a single letter, like Sūrah Qāf, or Sūrah Qalam. Some have two letters, like Sūrah Yā Sīn, and some have more. We will never know their true meaning, but our scholars have given over fifteen opinions as to why Allāh revealed the disjointed letters at the beginning of some sūrahs.

What is noteworthy is that almost every time Allāh begins a sūrah with one or more disjointed letters, the next verse praises the Qur'ān. Some scholars have, therefore, deduced that the *ḥurūf al-muqaṭṭa'āt* denote the majesty of the Qur'ān. The early scholars noticed that the *ḥurūf al-muqaṭṭa'āt* use fourteen letters of the Arabic alphabet, precisely half of the total. Some scholars contended that through these letters, Allāh challenged the Quraysh by indicating that the Qur'ān is composed of letters from the alphabet of their language, yet they are unable to produce anything like it.

There are five 'Verses of Challenge' in the Qur'ān, in which Allāh dares the disbelievers to produce something similar to it. He says, *'If all humans and jinn were to come together to produce the equivalent of this Qur'ān, they could not produce its equal, no matter how they supported each other.'*[4] In other verses, we find, *'...produce ten sūrahs like it...'*[5] and *'...produce one sūrah like it...'*[6] There may be a linkage between the *ḥurūf al-muqaṭṭa'āt* and these 'Verses of Challenge', proving that the Qur'ān is inimitable.

'...These are the verses...' *Tilka* is a definite Arabic article which means 'this or these,' and is used to denote something that is far away, in contrast to the word *hādhīhī,* which indicates a near object. Why does Allāh reference the Qur'ān with a pronoun that denotes something far away when the Qur'ān is in our hands? The scholars say that this is to show us the status of the Qur'ān as something exalted. The Qur'ān is not 'far away' physically, but it is majestic and noble and, therefore, transcendent in status.

The fact that here Allāh calls them 'verses or *āyāt* ' and in other places sūrah, as in–*'Whenever a sūrah is revealed...'*–shows that it is He Who divided the Qur'ān into parts. Many other scriptures, including the New Testament, have human-made divisions. An *āyah* also means a sign, an indication, or a miracle. Allāh calls the miracle of creation an *āyah,* and the verses of the Qur'ān an *āyah,* to signify

4 *al-Isrā* (17: 88).
5 *Hūd* (11: 13).
6 *Yūnus* (10:38).

the eloquence of the Qur'ānic language. Every verse of the Qur'ān has a message, and every verse is a miracle.

'...of the clear Book.' The phrase *'kitab mubīn'* occurs quite a few times in the Qur'ān. The word *mubīn* means 'clear', and it is a description of the Book or *Kitāb*. Allāh refers to the Qur'ān by many names, and the two most common are *Kitāb* and Qur'ān. They complement each other's meaning: the K*itāb* is the Revelation in writing, whereas the Qur'ān is its oral form meant for recitation. The Qur'ān is written down and recited simultaneously. It was written down by the commandment of Allāh, Who also recited it to archangel Jibrīl. Allāh has preserved the Qur'ān through both mediums. Other religious texts were written down by scribes long after the time of their prophets, and today the original message, for the most part, is lost.

The word *mubīn* could have two connotations. The first is that the Qur'ān is a clear Book, as declared at the beginning of Sūrah al-Baqarah, *'This is the Book! There is no doubt about it...,'* meaning there is no ambiguity in this Book. It means that anybody, rich or poor, who approaches the Qur'ān, will be able to receive its message. No doubt, the interpretation requires knowledge, but simple guidance can be obtained immediately, by anyone, even from a translation. In this sense, the Book is *mubīn* (clear).

Another possible meaning of *kitāb mubīn* is that, given its miraculous nature, it should be clear as day that it is from Allāh. Under this meaning, *mubīn* refers to the source of the Book – Allāh Himself. There is no other religious text that is as unambiguous and demarcated from beginning to end, as the Qur'ān. Allāh says, *'It is certainly We Who have revealed the Reminder, and it is certainly We Who will preserve it.'*[7] To this day, nobody knows who wrote the Bible. The New Testament was authored by anonymous people, two or three generations after the time of the Prophet ʿĪsā. Similarly, the authorship of the Old Testament is completely shrouded in mystery. Orthodox Jews believe that the Prophet Musā wrote it, but the Old Testament itself mentions the death of Musā and those who buried him, so this seems to be highly doubtful. Furthermore, no serious researcher believes that this work was authored by one person; there are too many indications of multiple authorships over the course of a few centuries. The Qur'ān, whatever belief one may have of it, is in a league of its own with regards to preservation, style and content.

To summarize, the Qur'ān is *kitāb mubīn* because its origin and source are known, and its message, verses, and words are clearly understood by those who sincerely desire to understand it.

إِنَّآ أَنزَلْنَٰهُ قُرْءَٰنًا عَرَبِيًّا لَّعَلَّكُمْ تَعْقِلُونَ ﴿٢﴾

Indeed, We have sent it down as an Arabic Qur'ān, so that you may understand.

People often wonder why Allāh refers to Himself in the plural when He says, '*...**We have**...*' There are two primary interpretations of this. First, the word 'We' is a royal plural, denoting Majesty, Honour, and Power. Kings and queens

[7] *al-Ḥijr* (15: 9).

throughout history have addressed themselves as such, and if anyone deserves the royal 'We,' it is Allāh.

Ibn Taymiyyah (d. 1328) had another interpretation. He said that every time the Qur'ān uses 'We', it is a reference to both Allāh and His angels. He cites several examples, *'And We send down blessed rain from the sky…'*[8] and, *'…We sent against them a furious wind…'*[9] because the angels bring the wind and rain. *'…We have revealed to you the Book…'*[10] because the Book came down with Jibrīl. On the other hand, when Allāh refers to worship, He always uses singular, *'It is truly I. I am Allāh! There is no god 'worthy of worship' except Me. So worship Me 'alone', and establish prayer for My remembrance.'*[11] This interpretation seems to be sound.

'…***sent it down*** …' The word used here is *anzala,* meaning 'to cause to descend' all at once. In other verses, the verb used for the Qur'ān is *nazzala,* which means to send it down in parts. Both verbs indicate that the Qur'ān came down physically, but the difference between the two is profound.

The Qur'ān came down with Jibrīl, and he then recited it to the Prophet ﷺ. We learn from a hadith in the *Mustadrak* of al-Ḥākim that on *Laylat al-Qadr* (The Night of Decree) Allāh physically sent down a Divine copy of the Qur'ān from the *Lawh al-Mahfūdh* (The Preserved Tablet). According to that narration, when Allāh says, *'Indeed, It is We 'Who' sent this 'Qur'ān' down on the Night of Decree,'*[12]

---

8 *Qāf* (50: 9).
9 *Fuṣṣilat* (41: 16).
10 *al-Naḥl* (16: 89).
11 *Tā Hā* (20:14).
12 *al-Qadr* (97: 1).

it refers to the entire Qur'ān being sent down from *al-Lawḥ al-Maḥfūdh* to the lowest heavens before the revelation began.[13] So, there is a physical descent of a Divine copy of the Qur'ān, and a metaphysical descent, meaning that the Qur'ān was within Jibrīl when he brought it down. It is one of the many proofs that Allāh is above us in a manner that befits Him because if He were not above us, the Qur'ān would not need to come down, nor would the Prophet ﷺ have to ascend to the heavens on the Night of *Miʿrāj*. So, the Qur'ān came down in its entirety on *Laylat al-Qadr to the lowest heaven,* which is *anzala, and then* Jibrīl brought it down in parts to the Prophet ﷺ over twenty-three years, which is *nazzala*.

*'...**as an Arabic Qur'ān...**'* Ten other verses describe the Qur'ān as being Arabic, and because of this, there is unanimity among scholars that only the Arabic Qur'ān constitutes Allāh's final revelation. A translation of the Qur'ān–and there are many–is not Allāh's Book. Allāh revealed the Qur'ān to an Arab prophet who lived in an Arabic-speaking community. Mainstream Muslims believe that the Qur'ān is *kalāmullāh* (the Speech of Allāh), and that Allāh spoke and recited the Qur'ān to Jibrīl. When He says, *'We have sent it down as an Arabic Qur'ān,'* it means that He recited it in Arabic. There is a continuous chain of recitation from Allāh, to Jibrīl, to the Prophet ﷺ, to the *Ṣaḥābah* and us. Because of this, when we recite the Qur'ān, we feel the Divine nature of the speech, even if we don't understand

[13] *Mustadrak* of al-Ḥākim (2879).

the meaning. This phenomenon is possible only because the Qur'ān is the Speech of Allāh.

'...so that you may understand.' Because Allāh does not specify here what we may understand, it leaves room for many interpretations. Allāh chose the language of the Arabs for this Revelation because it facilitates understanding. The Qur'ānic Arabic (*fuṣḥā*) is one of the most eloquent, and this should inspire us to learn it. Because Arabic is the language of the Qur'ān and *Sunnah,* it is an integral part of our religion, and learning it facilitates our access to it. As we will see in this *tafsīr,* an understanding of the Arabic of the Qur'ān provides the key to unlocking its deeper meaning.

Why does Allāh begin this sūrah by mentioning that He revealed the Qur'ān to the Prophet ﷺ? One of the reasons is to remind the Prophet ﷺ of the favours that Allāh has bestowed upon him. It is a common motif in the Qur'ān, for example, Allāh says, *'Your Lord 'O Prophet' has not abandoned you, nor has He become hateful 'of you'.'*[14] We find the reminders of Allāh's favours upon the Prophet ﷺ scattered throughout the Qur'ān, such as in Sūrahs al-Fatḥ, al-Aḥzāb, al-Qalam, and al-Inshirāḥ, to name a few. Allāh does this to console the Prophet ﷺ in times of hardship. And the greatest blessing Allāh has conferred upon His Prophet ﷺ is the revelation of the Qur'ān. As the Prophet's *Ummah*, we, too, are beneficiaries of this blessing.

---

14 *al-Ḍuḥā* (93: 3).

نَحْنُ نَقُصُّ عَلَيْكَ أَحْسَنَ ٱلْقَصَصِ بِمَآ أَوْحَيْنَآ إِلَيْكَ هَٰذَا ٱلْقُرْءَانَ
وَإِن كُنتَ مِن قَبْلِهِۦ لَمِنَ ٱلْغَٰفِلِينَ ﴿٣﴾

We relate to you 'O Prophet' the best of stories through Our revelation of this Qur'ān, though before this, you were totally unaware 'of them'.

Allāh used the plural *naḥnu* here, to refer to Himself and the angels. He said, ***'We relate to you 'O Prophet' the best of stories...'*** The word for story is *'qiṣṣah'*, which comes from *qaṣṣa*, meaning to follow footsteps in the sand. When the Bedouins found somebody's footsteps, they would follow them to catch up with that person. Allāh says about the Prophet Mūsā and Yūshaʿ bin Nūn, *'So they returned, retracing their footsteps...(qaṣaṣa).'*[15] What does a story have to do with following footsteps? Because by listening to someone's story, one walks in their footsteps. In other words, retracing someone's life is following them.

Everybody loves a good story. When we put children to sleep, we tell them a story, and this is what they love. But all of us are children in this regard: we all love to listen to stories. When we read a book about public speaking, we usually find a chapter on storytelling, because that is what makes a speaker effective. When a speaker begins a lecture with a personal anecdote or story, it grabs our attention.

Stories also teach memorable lessons; that is why the prophets used parables to drive a point home. When we

---

15 *al-Kahf* (18: 64).

hear the story of the Companions and how they reacted to the trials of their lives, we understand what it means to be patient. Stories teach us how to put our theology and faith into action. Upon hearing the story of the Prophet Ibrāhīm's trust in Allāh when the disbelievers threw him into the fire, we learn how Allāh protects His sincere servants. Stories inspire us, and their lessons remain ingrained in our souls. The fact that Allāh tells us stories in the Qur'ān is the greatest proof of their importance in teaching lessons.

Stories also serve as *'ibrah* (lesson) and warning that if we do not take heed, then a calamity that befell the people of the past can befall us because Allāh's *Sunnah* does not change. The lessons that Allāh teaches us are permanent and lasting, and there is much benefit to be gained from them. Hearing these stories reinforces our *īmān*. One of the fundamental lessons from the story of Yūsuf is that evil can never succeed, and righteousness will always prevail. Allāh says, *'And We relate to you, 'O Prophet,' the stories of the messengers to reassure your heart.'*[16]. Allāh strengthened the heart of the Prophet ﷺ with the story of the Prophet Yūsuf, and similarly, reading the stories of the prophets, and the *Sīrah* of the Prophet Muhammad ﷺ will strengthen our own.

Allāh relating the best of stories has two meanings. One, that every Qur'ānic story is the best of its kind because Allāh chose and narrated it; that it is a true story,

16 *Hūd* (11: 120).

not legend or fable; and that it has morals that Allāh taught most eloquently and wisely. Two, that out of all the excellent stories in the Qur'ān, the story of Yūsuf is the best because Allāh said so: *'We relate to you 'O Prophet' the best of stories…'*

'…through Our revelation of this Qur'ān, though before this, you were totally unaware 'of them'.' This verse is reminding the Prophet ﷺ that this story is of the blessings 'through this revelation We have given you: the Qur'ān.' The Prophet ﷺ did not know the past or the future, except for what Allāh told him, and of the countless stories, Allāh included in the Qur'ān only those that were most beneficial. Reminding the Prophet ﷺ that he was among the 'unaware', or *'ghāfilīn'* about the story of Yūsuf can mean several things: that Allāh is bestowing a favour by telling him this story, and that it is proof that he is a prophet and did not write the Qur'ān himself. In Arabic, a *ghāfil* is someone who does not know, and *ghafla* means a state of unknowing. *Ghafla* can be both intentional and unintentional. In the Prophet's case, it was involuntary because he ﷺ did not know the details of this story before Sūrah Yūsuf came down. The Prophet ﷺ, who lived in Makkah without access to Jews or Christians or their Books, could not have known the story of Yūsuf had it not been for Allāh informing him. Therefore, this does not indicate that he is being criticized, for he couldn't possibly have known of this story. Rather, it indicates Allah's blessings on him in revealing this story.

إِذْ قَالَ يُوسُفُ لِأَبِيهِ يَـٰٓأَبَتِ إِنِّى رَأَيْتُ أَحَدَ عَشَرَ كَوْكَبًا
وَٱلشَّمْسَ وَٱلْقَمَرَ رَأَيْتُهُمْ لِى سَـٰجِدِينَ ﴿٤﴾

'Remember' when Yūsuf said to his father, "O, my dear father! Indeed, I dreamt of eleven stars, and the sun, and the moon; I saw them prostrating to me!"

'Remember when…' The word *idh* occurs frequently in the Qur'ān right before a story begins, and in English, it means 'remember when'. It is simply the most common way that stories were begun back then.

'…Yūsuf said to his father…' Yūsuf was the son of Ya'qūb (Jacob), who was the son of Isḥāq (Isaac), who was the son of Ibrāhīm (Abraham). Four generations of prophets: this is truly a noble lineage! The Prophet Muhammad ﷺ was asked who the most noble person was in terms of lineage, and he replied: 'The noble, son of the noble, son of the noble, son of the noble one was Yūsuf ibn Ya'qūb ibn Isḥāq ibn Ibrāhīm.'[17] In lineage, no one can surpass Yūsuf.

The story of Yūsuf's great-grandfather Ibrāhīm is well known. He was one of the greatest prophets and whose legacy more than half of humanity follows today. Ibrāhīm beseeched Allāh for righteous children, and Allāh blessed him with his first son, Ismā'īl (Ishmael), from his maidservant Hajar (Hagar) when he was in his old age.

---

17 *Al-Adab Al-Mufrad* of Imam al-Bukhārī (896).

When Ismāʿīl was a teenager, Allāh blessed Ibrāhīm with a second son, Isḥāq, from his wife Sāra (Sarah). Ismāʿīl became the father of the Arabs, and Isḥāq became the father of the Jews through his son, Yaʿqūb. The Children of Israel come from Yaʿqūb, whose other name was Isrā'īl. Ismāʿīl's progeny had no prophets other than our Prophet Muḥammad ﷺ. The Prophet Ibrāhīm made *duʿā'* to Allāh, *'Our Lord! Make us both 'fully' submit to You, and from our descendants, a nation that will submit to You.'*[18] Allāh granted Ibrāhīm's prayer and gave him through Ismāʿīl the greatest prophet, Muhammad ﷺ. All other prophets came from the lineage of Isḥāq in a continuous chain, culminating in ʿĪsā (Jesus), to guide the Children of Israel. In Sūrah Baqarah, Allāh reminded the Jews of His blessings, saying, *'O Children of Israel! Remember 'all' the favours I granted you and how I honoured you above the others.'*[19]

Muslim scholars recommend that our discussion of the life of the prophets should rely on information found in the Qur'ān and *Sunnah* as much as possible. Looking at other sources, in particular, the Old and New Testaments is not forbidden *per se*, but it is problematic because one may never be sure of their authenticity. We may use them as additional reference points, but not base our creed on them or derive legal rulings from them. The Prophet ﷺ said, 'When you narrate from the Children of Israel, neither believe it nor deny it.'[20]

[18] *al-Baqarah* (2: 128).
[19] *al-Baqarah* (2: 47).
[20] *Ṣaḥīḥ* al-Bukhārī (3461).

According to reports in the Old Testament, the Prophet Ya'qūb had four consorts, two of whom were wives and two maidservants. From them, he had twelve sons. Yūsuf and his full brother Binyāmīn (Benjamin) were from one wife, Rāḥīl (Rachel). The rest of the sons were from the three other wives. According to a majority of Muslims scholars, including Ibn 'Abbās, the mother of Yūsuf died while giving birth to Binyāmīn. Ya'qūb then married Rāḥīl's sister, Yūsuf 's aunt and now also the stepmother, who took care of Binyāmīn and Yūsuf.

As a young child, Yūsuf lived in Canān, in what is now known as Palestine and Syria, which was the Holy Land that Allāh chose for Isḥāq and his progeny. Most likely, it was Ya'qūb who built a mosque in Jerusalem (some say it was perhaps Isḥāq). This mosque would eventually be rebuilt during the time of Sulaymān (Solomon) as the Great Temple. The Prophet Ibrāhīm, the patriarch, had constructed the Ka'bah some years earlier. When the Prophet ﷺ was asked which mosque was built first, he replied, '*Al-Masjid al-Ḥarām* (in Makkah).' He was then asked which mosque was built next, he replied, '*Masjid al-Aqsa* (in Jerusalem).' Then he was asked how many years were between them, he said, 'Forty years.'[21] So Ibrāhīm and his progeny founded both Holy Lands: Ismā'īl (and his father) in Makkah and Isḥāq (or possibly his son) in Palestine.

'...Indeed, I dreamt...' Most scholars say that Yūsuf was around seven years old when this incident occurred.

21 *Ṣaḥīḥ* of al-Bukhārī (3365).

We learn from the Qur'ān and *Sunnah* that dreams fall into three categories: those that come from Allāh, those that come from *Shayṭān,* and those that come from one's imagination. True dreams come from Allāh, and they occur mostly to prophets, but sometimes to others as well. In a hadith in *Saḥīḥ* of al-Bukhārī, the Prophet ﷺ said that after him, 'Nothing is left of the prophethood except *al-Mubashshirāt*.' They asked, 'What are *al-Mubashshirāt*?' He replied, 'The true good dreams.'[22] This type of dream is *mubashshir* or good news. A prophet's dream is *waḥy* or inspiration from Allāh. Same was the case with Ibrāhīm's vision in which he saw that Allāh had ordered him to sacrifice his son, Ismāʿīl. (It should be noted that several early Muslim scholars believed that that sacrificial son was Isḥāq). Now Yūsuf also saw a prophetic dream.

'...of eleven stars, and the sun, and the moon; I saw them prostrating to me!' The verse has Yūsuf repeating the verb *raʿaytu* ('I saw') twice; from this, some have derived that when he first saw the eleven stars, the sun, and the moon, they were stationary, and then in the dream, they moved and prostrated to him. Yūsuf was a young child, and he could not understand the meaning of this dream, so he told his father what he saw.

The sun, the moon, and the stars are celestial bodies high above us. These objects that Yūsuf saw in his dream symbolized shining people, i.e., his parents and brothers. Even in English, we call somebody who is famous a 'star,' meaning they shine brightly and are worthy of being

[22] *Ṣaḥīḥ* of al-Bukhārī (6990).

followed. The fact that they prostrate indicates there is a being that is higher and nobler than all of them, and that is Yūsuf. Several Muslim scholars said the eleven stars represented Yūsuf's brothers and that the sun and the moon his parents, but a few other scholars opined that the sun symbolized the mother, and the moon the father because the right of the mother is three times that of the father. Yet others said that the sun represented Yaʿqūb and the moon Yūsuf's mother. Whichever the case, the dream showed that Yūsuf would eventually rise higher in rank than the other members of his family, including his father, the Prophet Yaʿqūb.

قَالَ يَٰبُنَيَّ لَا تَقْصُصْ رُءْيَاكَ عَلَىٰٓ إِخْوَتِكَ فَيَكِيدُوا۟ لَكَ كَيْدًا ۖ إِنَّ
ٱلشَّيْطَٰنَ لِلْإِنسَٰنِ عَدُوٌّ مُّبِينٌ ﴿٥﴾

He replied, "O, my dear son! Do not relate your vision to your brothers, or they will devise a plot against you. Surely Shayṭān is a sworn enemy to humankind."

When Yaʿqūb heard about the dream, he warned Yūsuf, ***'...Do not relate your vision to your brothers, or they will devise a plot against you...'*** There is a double emphasis here, and a translation won't do it justice. One of the problems of writing the Qur'ānic *tafsīr* in another language is that it loses much of the *balāghah* or elegance and rhetoric that are the hallmarks of the Arabic language. So, 'They will plot against you a very severe plot,' indicates that the plot would be powerful and effective.

Notice the first thing Ya'qūb said was, *'Do not tell your dream to others,'* because telling it could bring harm. Ya'qūb was also concerned to prevent jealousy amongst his sons. He was well aware of the nature of his children. Even though, as a father, he loved them all, he knew they were not all the same. He took active steps to maintain peace and harmony in his family and made sure that the siblings did not fall into dispute. What Ya'qūb did as a father, we should also emulate, not just with our family but also with extended relatives and friends. Our Prophet ﷺ said, 'A dream is like a bird flying; when it is interpreted, it lands. And it should not be narrated except to a concerned person, or an interpreter.'[23]

We also see that the parents' love for their child is selfless. The symbolism of the dream is that a day might come when Ya'qūb will prostrate to Yūsuf, meaning the son will surpass the father in status. Perhaps this is the only relationship where jealousy does not exist because a parent sees in the child their extension. When Yūsuf told his dream to Ya'qūb, he understood the implications but felt no resentment. Instead, his instinct told him to protect his son. It shows us the perfection of Allāh's creation.

This verse also reminds us that we should not flaunt our blessings. Doing so can cause people to become jealous. The dangers of jealousy and envy are a common theme throughout this sūrah, and we see them highlighted here.

---

23 *Sunan* of al-Tirmidhī (2278).

Jealousy is a burning desire to have what someone else has. It is a selfish and destructive desire that sees others as undeserving. It is a disease that occurs in both men and women, and generally speaking (although this is a stereotype, there is an element of general truth in it) men are jealous of wealth and power and women are jealous of beauty. This feeling of jealousy contradicts *īmān* in Allāh because it is as if someone is saying, 'O Allāh, why did You make her more beautiful? Or, 'O Allāh, why did You give him more money?' The Prophet ﷺ said, 'Beware of envy, for it devours good deeds just as fire devours wood or grass.'[24] It is an interesting hadith because jealousy is a feeling, and in Islam, the general rule is that we are not accountable for our feelings and thoughts until we act upon them. But here we see that some feelings are an exception to the rule, and harbouring them makes us liable. Jealousy is foremost amongst them, and if we don't empty our hearts of this vice, it will consume our good deeds.

'...Surely Shayṭān is a sworn enemy to humankind.' Yaʿqūb taught his son a beautiful lesson here: no matter who does the evil, *Shayṭān* is the one instigating and exacerbating it. It doesn't negate that a person is responsible for their actions, but it allows one to find a way out when another person does something wrong. Instead of placing the ultimate blame and guilt on fellow Muslims, we should blame the *Shayṭān* because he is our

[24] *Sunan* of Abū Dawūd (4903).

sworn enemy who persistently whispers evil ideas in us. Yaʿqūb told Yūsuf not to inform his brothers about the dream lest they became jealous and tried to harm him; then he warned him that *Shayṭān* was an open enemy. And even though he foresaw the ten half-brothers of Yūsuf plotting, he put the primary blame on *Shayṭān.* Yaʿqūb did not call Yūsuf's brothers 'enemies' or 'evil'. It is very profound because when it comes to criticizing others, it is an Islamic etiquette to remove the blame from the individual and transfer it to *Shayṭān* as much as possible. It opens the door for them to repent for their mistake and come closer to Allāh. However, there is one difference. When we criticize ourselves, we should not use *Shayṭān* as an excuse. Since Ādam, *Shayṭān* has been plotting our downfall. Allāh says in the Qur'ān, *'So We cautioned, "O Ādam! He is surely an enemy to you…"'*[25] *Shayṭān* is ever-eager to cause us to go astray. It's important to note that he doesn't have any control over us; he merely seeks to tempt us through a whisper. In the Qur'ān, Allāh tells us that on the Day of Judgement, people will blame *Shayṭān,* saying that it was he who caused them to go astray. But he will say, *'…Indeed, Allāh has made you a true promise. I, too, made you a promise, but I failed you. I did not have any authority over you. I only called you, and you responded to me. So do not blame me; blame yourselves…'*[26]

[25] *Ṭā Hā* (20: 117).

[26] *Ibrahīm* (14:22).

وَكَذَٰلِكَ يَجْتَبِيكَ رَبُّكَ وَيُعَلِّمُكَ مِن تَأْوِيلِ ٱلْأَحَادِيثِ وَيُتِمُّ نِعْمَتَهُۥ
عَلَيْكَ وَعَلَىٰٓ ءَالِ يَعْقُوبَ كَمَآ أَتَمَّهَا عَلَىٰٓ أَبَوَيْكَ مِن قَبْلُ إِبْرَٰهِيمَ
وَإِسْحَٰقَ ۚ إِنَّ رَبَّكَ عَلِيمٌ حَكِيمٌ ﴿٦﴾

And so, will your Lord choose you 'O Yūsuf', and teach you the interpretation of dreams, and perfect His favour upon you and the descendants of Yaʿqūb, 'just' as He once perfected it upon your fathers, Ibrāhīm and Isḥāq. Surely your Lord is All-Knowing, All-Wise.

When Allāh says, ***'And so, will your Lord…'*** it could mean either, 'through this dream' Allāh will protect you, or 'through you not telling others about it' the protection will come. If Yūsuf had told the dream to his brothers, much worse could have happened. Allāh then says, ***'…choose you…'*** which comes from *ijtiba,* literally meaning, 'to sift through and find the best'. And He will, '…***teach you the interpretation of dreams…'*** showing us that the knowledge of interpretation of dreams is a pure blessing from Allāh.

'…and perfect His favour upon you and the descendants of Yaʿqūb...' Notice that Yūsuf is mentioned separately from his brethren, signifying that his blessings were equivalent to all of them combined. Yūsuf is in a category of his own. Allāh bestowed many blessings upon Yūsuf, among them: prophethood; noble lineage; elevated above his brothers;

the interpretation of dreams; half of all beauty; and the good fortune of admission into *Jannah*.

In the Qur'ān, the family of Yaʿqūb is called *al-Asbāṭ* (the Patriarchs). The brothers of Yūsuf also became prophets. So, it begs the question: how could prophets plot a grievous crime? The majority of scholars said that when this incident occurred, the brothers had not yet become prophets. How do we know that they eventually did become prophets? Because Allāh says, *'Say, 'O believers,' 'We believe in Allāh and what was revealed to us, and Ibrāhīm and Ismāʿīl and Isḥāq and Yaʿqūb and the Asbāṭ...'*[27] Who are the *Asbāṭ*? The sons of Yaʿqūb.

Another critical point here is that Allāh protects the children of His righteous servants, as we repeatedly learned in Sūrah Kahf. Therefore, one of the best ways to guarantee that Allāh protects our children and that they are righteous is for us to be pious ourselves. In Sūrah al-Kahf, when Khiḍr and Musā passed by the broken wall and Khiḍr stopped to rebuild it, Musā asked, 'What was the purpose of this?' At the end of the story, Khiḍr revealed, *'And as for the wall, it belonged to two orphan boys in the city, and under the wall was a treasure that belonged to them, and their father was a righteous man. So, your Lord willed that these children should come of age and retrieve their treasure as a mercy from your Lord.'*[28] The father was righteous, and because of that, Allāh blessed his children in this world and the next.

---

[27] *al-Baqarah* (2: 136).
[28] *al-Kahf* (18: 82).

Allāh then says, ***'...'just' as He once perfected it upon your fathers, Ibrāhīm and Isḥāq...'*** What are the favours that Allāh bestowed on Ibrāhīm? They are truly worthy of a book. He was the father of all nations and all prophets that came after him; he was blessed with prophethood when there were no other Muslims on earth; he was the first *khalīlullāh*[29] (Friend of Allāh); Allāh saved him from the fire of King Nimrod in this world, and will protect him from the Fire of Jahannam in the next.

'...Surely your Lord is All-Knowing, All-Wise.' Allāh concludes this verse by using two of His Beautiful Names: *Al-'Alīm* and *Al-Ḥakīm. Al-'Alīm* means the All-Knowing and *Al-Ḥakīm* incorporates two meanings: *hikmah,* meaning wisdom, and *ḥukm,* meaning judgement. Allāh is All-Wise and the Judge of all Judges. Why does Allāh end this verse with these particular attributes? It is as if He is saying, 'I know what I am doing. I do everything with wisdom. Realize that whatever is going to happen to you, I am *Al-Ḥakīm* and I have a Divine Plan. Don't despair. I know the past, and I know the future. Just like I saved your grandfather Isḥāq from being slaughtered,[30] and your great-grandfather Ibrāhīm from the fire, so shall I save you. I put them through trials, and I will put you through trials, but you shall emerge victorious just as they did. I am *Al-ʿAlīm* and *Al-Ḥakīm.*'

---

[29] The other *khalīlullah* was the Prophet Muhammad ﷺ.

[30] The majority opinion is that it was Ismāʿīl who was saved from the sacrifice. However, the opinion that it was Isḥāq who was saved from the 'sacrifice' was that of Imam al-Ṭabarī and some early authorities. And this reference of Yūsuf being blessed because his 'father' Isḥāq was 'saved' is therefore linked to this verse according to those scholars who held the sacrificial son to be Iṣḥāq.

لَّقَدْ كَانَ فِي يُوسُفَ وَإِخْوَتِهِۦٓ ءَايَٰتٌ لِّلسَّآئِلِينَ ۝٧

Indeed, in the story of Yusuf and his brothers there are lessons for all who ask.

The word translated as 'lessons' here is *āyah,* and as we have already highlighted, this means that it is a sign, a lesson, and a miracle to ponder over. In some places in the Qur'ān, Allāh says there are lessons for those who think, and in others, He calls them lessons for those who reflect and lessons for those who use their *ʿaql* (intellect). This verse is the only place in the Qur'ān, where Allāh says that these signs are lessons for those who 'ask'.

Allāh says, ***'...in the story of Yūsuf and his brothers, there are lessons for all who ask.'*** Asking is the rudimentary level of inquisitiveness, while thinking and contemplating indicate a deeper level of inquiry. The meaning here is that these *āyāt* are so clear, one does not even need to think deeply to understand them. All one needs to do is turn to the sūrah and ask, 'What are the miracles? What are the signs? How can I benefit from them?' The reason Sūrah Yūsuf appeals to so many of us is that it is straightforward and easy to understand.

Since an *āyah*, or lesson, is an indication, the scholars have said that Sūrah Yūsuf primarily points to three things: the Power of Allāh and His *Sunnah*, the Truth of the Messenger, and the lessons and morals within the story of Yūsuf. It shows us who Allāh is and how He deals with His servants. From it, we learn that Allāh is always watching over His servants, and in the end, victory will be for the sincere and righteous. The lesson is that righteousness shall always prevail. The reason for the revelation of this sūrah was to console the Prophet ﷺ during his grief and suffering. It told him that even though he was being ridiculed and humiliated, he would be victorious in the end, like Yūsuf, because this is the reward for those that have *taqwā*. The entire Sūrah Yūsuf is an *āyah* about the truthfulness of our beloved Prophet Muḥammad ﷺ. Allāh is saying that in this story, there is an *āyah* that this prophet is a true prophet because he would not have known this story otherwise. The following verse beautifully articulates this point: *'This is one of the stories of the unseen, which We reveal to you 'O Prophet'. Neither you nor your people knew it before this. So be patient! Surely the ultimate outcome belongs 'only' to the righteous.'*[31]

إِذْ قَالُوا۟ لَيُوسُفُ وَأَخُوهُ أَحَبُّ إِلَىٰٓ أَبِينَا مِنَّا وَنَحْنُ عُصْبَةٌ إِنَّ
أَبَانَا لَفِى ضَلَٰلٍ مُّبِينٍ ﴿٨﴾

'Remember' when they said 'to one another',
"Surely Yūsuf and his brother 'Binyāmīn'
are more beloved to our father than we, even
though we are a group of so many. Indeed,
our father is clearly mistaken."

Allāh begins this verse with, ***"'Remember' when they said: Surely Yūsuf and his brother…"*** There is a particular emphasis in the name of Yūsuf here (the extra *lām*) as if

31 *Hūd* (11: 49).

to say: 'This is an undeniable fact about Yūsuf and his brother.' They were all Yūsuf's brothers, but by unanimous consensus, here they are talking in the singular about his full brother, Binyāmīn. Yūsuf and Binyāmīn were the youngest and from the same mother. Binyāmīn was still a new-born baby at this stage, and Yūsuf, a young child.

Notice that they say, ***'...more beloved to our father...'*** They knew how much their father loved Yūsuf, but could not accuse him of giving Yūsuf more than the other children. In our *Sharīʿah,* we must treat our children equally. We cannot prefer one child over another in material blessings, and this is a critical theological point: the brothers only accused Yāqūb of loving Yūsuf and his brother more. A person has no control over love. Loving is an emotion of the heart, and Allāh does not call one to account for loving one of their children more.

Once a man came to the Prophet ﷺ and said, 'Bear witness that I have given my son Nu'mān such and such from my wealth.' He ﷺ said, 'Have you given all your children something like that which you have given to Nu'mān?' The man said, 'No.' The Prophet ﷺ said, 'Then let someone other than me bear witness to that. Would you not like all your children to honour you equally?' The man said, 'Of course.' The Prophet ﷺ said, 'Then do not do this.'[32]

'...than we, even though we are a group of so many...' The word used here for a group is *'uṣbah,* meaning a large number. They were ten brothers, and they tried to use their numerical strength in opposition to Yūsuf and his

32 *Sunan* of Ibn Mājah (2375).

full brother, who were just two. They also hinted that they were older and, therefore, more useful to their father in taking care of his needs.

'...Indeed, our father is clearly mistaken.' Once again, *inna* and *la* add emphasis here. 'Surely – there is no doubt – our father has made a clear grievous error.' Remember that Ya'qūb was a prophet. The sons did not say their father was in error concerning his faith in Islam; they alleged that he was misguided regarding his greater love for Yūsuf and Binyāmīn.

Immediately we can see that the brothers were not as righteous as Yūsuf; otherwise, they would not have spoken like this. We notice here that a father has a greater love for more righteous children, and that is why Yūsuf's brothers were jealous.

ٱقْتُلُوا۟ يُوسُفَ أَوِ ٱطْرَحُوهُ أَرْضًا يَخْلُ لَكُمْ وَجْهُ أَبِيكُمْ
وَتَكُونُوا۟ مِنۢ بَعْدِهِۦ قَوْمًا صَٰلِحِينَ ٩

"Kill Yūsuf or cast him out to some 'distant' land so that our father's attention will be only ours, then after that, you may 'repent and' become righteous people!"

The brothers' jealousy was consuming them from inside, to the point that they decided to ***'Kill Yūsuf...'*** Their jealousy had impaired their thinking and driven them to insanity. Alas, they could not see that they were jealous of something noble.

They said, ***'...cast him out to some 'distant' land...'*** meaning some land we don't care about, far removed from us, ***'...so that our father's attention will be only ours.'*** They assumed, naively, that if they removed the object of their father's love, he would then shower all his love on them. What they didn't realize is that love exists in the heart, and at times, the absence of the beloved makes the heart grow fonder!

'...after that, you may 'repent, and' become righteous people!' The brothers had used an interesting phrase here. They were saying, 'Let's do the heinous deed, and then after that, we can become good people.' These thoughts were clearly from *Shayṭān,* who made their evil plot appear justified to them, saying, 'Don't worry, you can just atone for it afterwards.' *Shayṭān* has been deluding people like this since the beginning of time. The brothers didn't realize that once they committed the crime, they would need to lie to cover it up, and then swear upon that lie. One wrong action is never the end of the story, and through the story of Yūsuf, Allāh warns us about this tactic of *Shayṭān.*

Some commentators of the Qur'ān said that the brothers were still young and hadn't reached puberty. In Islam, children are not accountable for their deeds. Others refuted this idea and said that the brothers of Yūsuf were adults when they committed the crime because this verse shows us that if they had still been children, they would not be thinking in this manner. Those who said that the brothers were not yet adults used the phrase '*...let us play*', and claimed that adults would not be asking to play. Hence, they argue, they were still children. The response from the majority of interpreters was that adults do indeed play and are allowed to be merry! Even ʿĀ'ishah and the Prophet ﷺ played sometimes, as in the famous incident of the two of them racing one another in the desert.. The opinion that the brothers were adults gets support from the end of the story, where they said, *'O our father! Pray for the forgiveness of our sins. We have certainly been sinful.'*[33] Had they been children, they would not have had to ask for forgiveness because a child is not accountable to Allāh for his misdeeds.

Another interesting point this verse brings is that the brothers intended to do a nefarious deed followed by a good deed so that Allāh would forgive them. In terms of this *dunyā*, their motivation was that if they removed Yūsuf, their father's attention would turn to them. They lost both objectives. The first goal was to make one mistake and then become good after that, but that one mistake led to another and then another. The second goal was to get their father's attention, but their father turned away from them in his grief. Had Yūsuf been there, their father would have loved the other children to a reasonable degree; by depriving their father of Yūsuf, they broke his heart, thereby reducing his capacity to love them. So they neither achieved their worldly goal nor were they able to achieve the spiritual one of being righteous, until they completely repented and confessed their sins. Disobeying Allah brings neither bodily nor spiritual blessings!

An important lesson we derive from the story of the brothers of Yūsuf is that we should not resort to ignoble

33 *Yūsuf* (12: 97).

means to achieve a noble goal. The brothers wanted something *halal*: the love of their father. But the way they approached it was *ḥarām*. The brothers wanted their father to stop doting on Yūsuf, but their actions created the opposite effect: his love and longing for Yūsuf only intensified.

However, one positive aspect may be derived from this story. Since the brothers plotted a dastardly deed with the aim to repent later, some of our scholars have said that their attitude was better than that of a person who had no qualms about committing a crime. The brothers hoped, 'Allāh will forgive us,' and in the end, He did, as Allāh's Mercy is vast, and He is the Most Forgiving and the Most Merciful. While that attitude is not an excuse for them, it is most certainly better than the criminal who commits a crime without a shred of remorse.

قَالَ قَآئِلٌ مِّنْهُمْ لَا تَقْتُلُواْ يُوسُفَ وَأَلْقُوهُ فِى غَيَٰبَتِ ٱلْجُبِّ
يَلْتَقِطْهُ بَعْضُ ٱلسَّيَّارَةِ إِن كُنتُمْ فَٰعِلِينَ ١٠

One of them said, "Do not kill Yūsuf. But if you must do something, throw him into the bottom of a well so perhaps he may be picked up by some travelers."

Some scholars have said that it was the eldest brother who said this because he will appear again later in the story. No doubt, the one speaking here had more intelligence and piety than the others. In his perfect wisdom, Allāh does not give us more detail than we need. If we read the Old

Testament or any book of history, we quickly get bored because there are too many irrelevant details. The beauty of the Qur'ānic stories is that we never get bored or bogged down in extra details.

'...Do not kill Yūsuf. But if you must do something...' The brother who disagreed with the idea of murder did not vigorously oppose it either. He merely tried to minimize the harm. They wanted to kill Yūsuf or exile him to the desert, but this brother suggested that they throw him in a well so that somebody will eventually pull him out. He reasoned that this way Yūsuf would likely become a slave, but would at least live. Suggesting the lesser of two evils is a well-known principle in our religion. There is a rule in the science of jurisprudence, or *usūl al-fiqh* that if one must choose between two *ḥarām* options, let them select the lesser *ḥarām*.

Notice here that Allāh is describing the evil deeds of the brothers, and they are numerous. They are breaking the ties of kinship. Yūsuf is not just their brother, he is a younger brother, and they are breaking the bonds of a young child with his father. They are also violating the rights of their father. The Prophet ﷺ said in a beautiful hadith, 'Whoever does not show mercy to our young ones, or acknowledge the rights of our elders, is not one of us.'[34] Through their crime, the brothers disobeyed both commands. Also, because Ya'qūb, their father, is a prophet of Allāh, their sins are magnified.

All of this highlights the dangers of *ḥasad*, or envy and jealousy. The Prophet ﷺ said, 'There has come to you the

[34] *Musnad* of Imam Aḥmad (7033).

disease of the nations before you, jealousy and hatred. It is the 'shaver' (destroyer); I do not say that it shaves hair, but that it shaves faith.'[35] The shaving of the religion here means that *ḥasad* gradually erodes one's faith until nothing is left. The Prophet ﷺ also said, 'By the One in Whose Hand my soul is, you will not enter Paradise until you believe, and you will not believe until you love one another. Shall I not tell you of that which will strengthen the love between you? Spread (the greeting of) *salām* amongst yourselves.'[36] Planting love in the hearts by spreading the *salām* is the opposite of *ḥasad*.

'...throw him into the bottom of a well, so perhaps he may be picked up by some travelers.' The word *ghayāb* used in this verse means 'a recess' or the bottom of the well, and it comes from *ghayb*, meaning the 'unseen'. They also use the word *jubb* to describe the well, rather than the more common, *bi'r*; this is because *jubb* indicates a primitive well that doesn't have a built wall around it, while *bi'r* is a properly constructed well. The brother said, 'throw him into the bottom of a *jubb*,' which means he knew which type of well it was. It was a rudimentary well that was probably infrequently used, and lay in an isolated place visited by travelers only. The brothers said that some 'travelers' might 'pick up' or 'find' Yūsuf as if he would be something unexpected for them. The words are precise, and the brothers are well aware of the nefariousness of their plot.

---

35 *Sunan* of al-Tirmidhī (2434).

36 *Ṣaḥīḥ* of Imam Muslim (54).

قَالُوا۟ يَـٰٓأَبَانَا مَالَكَ لَا تَأْمَ۫نَّا عَلَىٰ يُوسُفَ وَإِنَّا لَهُۥ لَنَـٰصِحُونَ ﴿١١﴾

They said, "O our father! Why do you not trust us with Yūsuf, although we truly wish him well?"

The brothers had agreed that they would take Yūsuf and throw him into the well, but they knew that their father would be suspicious, so they thought carefully about how to present their request. They said, ***'O our father! Why do you not trust us with Yūsuf...'*** then they tried to avoid suspicion by adding, ***'...although we truly wish him well?'*** They sought to reassure Ya'qūb, essentially saying, 'Surely, we are his well-wishers (*nāṣiḥūn*).' *Naṣahah* means to want good for somebody. *Naṣīḥa,* which means to give advice, also comes from this root because the purpose behind *naṣīḥa* is good of the advisee. From the wording, we can infer that until this point, the brothers did not have an opportunity to take Yūsuf on an outing. Perhaps this meant that Ya'qūb was cautious and did not trust them.

أَرْسِلْهُ مَعَنَا غَدًا يَرْتَعْ وَيَلْعَبْ وَإِنَّا لَهُۥ لَحَـٰفِظُونَ ﴿١٢﴾

"Send him out with us tomorrow so that he may enjoy himself and play. And we will surely watch over him."

The brothers tried to calm and reassure their father, disarming his suspicion and showing him that they were sincere.

Then the petition came: ***'Send him with us tomorrow,*** **so** ***that he may enjoy himself and play…'*** To play or have a good time is permissible in our religion as long as it does not cause us to neglect our duties. Allāh refers to *laʿib* or 'play' here. *Laʿib* and *lahu* are two different things, and Allāh mentions both of them when He described this world as being *'play and amusement'.*[37] What is the difference between the two? *Laʿib* is something that is not highly beneficial but is permissible in small quantities, whereas *lahu* has no benefit in it whatsoever. *Laʿib* is something the Prophet ﷺ occasionally did, like when racing with ʿĀ'ishah or playing with Ḥasan and Ḥusayn. There is a narration that during the days of Mina, Abū Bakr came to ʿĀ'ishah, while there were two girls with her, playing the *duff* (drum) and singing. The Prophet ﷺ was lying nearby covered in his garment. Abū Bakr rebuked the two girls, but the Prophet ﷺ uncovered his face and said, 'O Abu Bakr! Leave them, for these are the days of 'Id.' Once, in the *masjid* of the Prophet ﷺ, the Abyssinians demonstrated their spear-throwing skills. The *Ṣaḥābah* were watching them, and ʿĀ'ishah wanted to see as well, so the Prophet ﷺ stood to allow her to watch from behind his shoulders. What is noteworthy is that this show of martial arts happened in the Mosque of the Prophet ﷺ. ʿĀ'ishah narrated, 'I was being screened by the Prophet ﷺ while I was watching the Ethiopians playing in the mosque. 'Umar rebuked them, but the Prophet ﷺ said, 'Leave them, O Banī Arfīda [meaning the Abyssinians]! Play, as you are safe.'[38] *Lahu,* on the other hand, would be something that

---

[37] *al-Anām* (6: 32).
[38] *Ṣaḥīḥ* of al-Bukharī (3529).

is a complete waste of time and not encouraged in our religion; for example, gambling.

The brothers' outward reason for wanting to take out Yūsuf to play was a form of emotional blackmail as if they were saying to their father, 'We are going to have a fun time; don't you want Yūsuf to enjoy? If you truly love Yūsuf, you'll send him with us.' First, they made him feel guilty by saying, 'Why don't you trust us? We are his brothers. What is your problem?' Now they added the icing to the cake, 'Don't you want Yūsuf to be happy?'

To emphasize their point, they said, ***'...And we will surely watch over him.'*** The Arabic word used here is precise; it is the same word Allāh used when He promised to protect the Qur'ān, *'Surely We revealed the Message, and We will be its guardian.'*[39] In Arabic, there are different levels of emphasizing a point, and the triple emphasis is the highest, which is used in this instance. The brothers were speaking eloquently with a tinge of emotion, and they appeared to be sincere. They had already plotted and planned, and they were now convincing their father, saying, 'Trust us; Yūsuf is going to be fine. We love him; he is our brother. Let him go and have fun. We will take care of him. We want his best interest. We are his elders, and we will protect him.'

In the face of the brothers' earnest and soulful request, Yaʿqūb could have just agreed, but there is something in his heart – an intuition – that is preventing him. In Arabic, the word for intuition is *firāsah,* a profound concept that

[39] *al-Ḥijr* (15: 9).

we will see come up again and again in Sūrah Yūsuf. The Prophet ﷺ said, 'Beware of the *firāsah* of a believer, for he sees with the light of Allāh.'[40] What does *firāsah* mean? We can translate it as a gut instinct, a sixth sense, or a spiritual intuition. Here, Yaʿqūb knew that something was wrong. He could have thought, after this beautiful introduction from his children, 'What excuse do I have?' But still, he hesitated, because his heart was not convinced. Not once had he allowed Yūsuf to be alone with the brothers, without supervision. As a last attempt to decline the request, Yaʿqūb used one final ploy.

قَالَ إِنِّي لَيَحْزُنُنِيٓ أَن تَذْهَبُواْ بِهِۦ وَأَخَافُ أَن يَأْكُلَهُ ٱلذِّئْبُ وَأَنتُمْ عَنْهُ غَٰفِلُونَ ﴿١٣﴾

He responded, "It would truly sadden me if you took him away with you, and I fear that a wolf may devour him while you are negligent of him."

Yaʿqūb said, ***'...It would truly sadden me if you took him away with you...'*** He could not bear to be away from Yūsuf, even for one day, but there is also a deeper meaning here. The brothers wanted to take Yūsuf for a day, but there is a subtle hint that he will be away for a long time.

---

[40] *Sunan* at-Tirmidhī (3127).

'...and I fear that a wolf may devour him while you are negligent of him.' Some scholars have said that Canān, where Yaʿqūb lived, was a desert wilderness, where wild beasts roamed, and that there was an ever-present danger of a wolf attacking Yūsuf or even his brothers. But other scholars differed: did Yaʿqūb truly mean that he was scared of a wolf, or was this just an excuse? The strongest opinion seems to be that Yaʿqūb was not worried about wolves; he was trying to find a reason to prevent the brothers from taking Yūsuf. What Yaʿqūb said about the wolf could be called a *tawriyah,* which Islam permits. A *tawriyah* is a statement or expression that could have more than one meaning. What the speaker says is technically correct, but the listener could understand it in a way that was not the former's intent. There was one chance in a million that a wolf could eat Yūsuf; what Yaʿqūb meant was, 'I don't want you to take him away,' but since he couldn't verbalize that excuse, he used a far less likely one to hide the real reason.

Ironically, Yaʿqūb gave the brothers the exact excuse that they would use later: 'a wolf ate Yūsuf'. It shows us that these young men were not mature enough even to plan out the whole plot. They were short-sighted and hadn't thought of what they were going to say afterwards. When Yaʿqūb verbalized this fear, they added it to their plan and used it against him. It shows us that the brothers of Yūsuf, like most criminals or people who sin, didn't think three steps ahead.

قَالُوا۟ لَئِنْ أَكَلَهُ ٱلذِّئْبُ وَنَحْنُ عُصْبَةٌ إِنَّآ إِذًا لَّخَـٰسِرُونَ ﴿١٤﴾

They said, "If a wolf were to devour him, despite our strong group, then we would certainly be losers!"

Allāh had decreed that the brothers would later use Ya'qūb's very excuse to feign Yūsuf's death. They said, how could a wolf devour their little brother, *'...**despite our strong group...?'*** The brothers were trying to assure Ya'qūb that even though he was an old man, they were a young and sturdy group; there is no way a wolf could attack a strong group like theirs. Ultimately, the sons prevailed; they won the emotional struggle, and Ya'qūb allowed Yūsuf to go with them.

PART TWO

Sold into Slavery

فَلَمَّا ذَهَبُواْ بِهِۦ وَأَجۡمَعُوٓاْ أَن يَجۡعَلُوهُ فِي غَيَٰبَتِ ٱلۡجُبِّۚ وَأَوۡحَيۡنَآ
إِلَيۡهِ لَتُنَبِّئَنَّهُم بِأَمۡرِهِمۡ هَٰذَا وَهُمۡ لَا يَشۡعُرُونَ ١٥

And so, when they took him away and decided to throw him into the bottom of the well, We inspired him: "'One day' you will remind them of this deed of theirs while they are unaware 'of who you are'."

With their ploy successful, the brothers spirited away Yūsuf from their father, heading straight into the wilderness. Allāh says, ***'...when they took him away...'*** without completing the statement. The Qur'ān often skips words, phrases, or details, and the scholars ascribe this to the *balāghah* or eloquence of the Arabic language. The Qur'ān uses the most comprehensive and concise speech that reflects Allāh's wisdom and knowledge. Details are glossed over, as shall be explained below.

He then says, ***'...and decided to throw him into the bottom of the well...'*** The brothers were unanimous about throwing Yūsuf into the well. There was not one merciful brother amongst them. We cannot even imagine what shock, fear, and horror Yūsuf must have felt. He had happily gone with the brothers to play and have fun, and here he was, looking in disbelief at them as they scurried to carry out their macabre plan.

Notice that Allāh did not explicitly criticize the brothers, despite their cruel act. Centuries later, when we think about it, our hearts still shudder, thinking, 'How could they have done that to a little brother?' Yet, Allāh does not use a single negative adjective in the sūrah to describe the brothers of Yūsuf, even though they were every bit worthy of criticism. Why? One of the main reasons is that it is not befitting for the Qur'ān's nobility to mention gore and evil, except in briefest terms. For example, to describe the factors that break one's ablution Allāh says in the Qur'ān, *'...or have relieved yourselves...,'*[41] rather than *'if one of you urinates or defecates.'* In yet another place, He says, *'...if you have touched your wives...'*[42] to describe marital relations. The words the Qur'ān uses are most dignifed and cultured.

The Qur'ān, therefore, teaches us a vital etiquette: be brief and dignified when mentioning evil. Although there are exceptions, it is discouraged for a Muslim to go into detail about someone's lewd or evil act, or sin. Allāh warns us in Sūrah Nūr, *'Indeed, those who love to see indecency spread among the believers will suffer a painful punishment in this life and the Hereafter.'*[43] We can see that Allāh's standards about morality and decency far surpass those set by humans. In modern societies, news outlets describe crime, vulgarity, murder, and rape in the most vivid detail using the most offensive language. Hollywood glorifies such subjects in blockbuster movies, and authors turn them into best-selling books. The tabloids have a field day with scandalous gossip. The preponderance of promiscuity desensitizes people, and, for some of them, the stories of

[41] *an-Nisā'* (4: 43).
[42] *an-Nisā'* (4: 43).
[43] *an-Nūr* (24: 19).

murder, illicit relationships, and the adoration of hedonistic lifestyles become a stepping-stone to committing those acts themselves.

Another reason for avoiding a detailed description of the crime and denunciation of the brothers is their repentance of the sin later. Allāh, the ever-forgiving, accepted their repentance. Amazingly, the only time the Qur'ān mentioned the brothers' transgression was through their own admission. In a remorseful tone, they said to Yūsuf, *'By Allāh! Allāh has truly preferred you over us, and we have surely been sinful.'*[44] And they said to their father, *'O our father! Pray for the forgiveness of our sins. We have certainly been guilty.'*[45] It is a compelling message. When Allāh has forgiven them, why mention their faults? Such graciousness only reflects Allāh's unparalleled forgiveness. True forgiveness means that we don't remind people about their mistakes or tell others about them.

Yūsuf was now at the bottom of a dark, secluded well. He's a young child, bewildered, frightened, and alone. It was part of Allāh's plan to put him in this situation, so He instilled *sakīnah*, or tranquillity, in his heart, and inspired to him, saying that, ***"'One day' you will remind them of this deed of theirs while they are unaware 'of who you are'."*** By using *tawkīd*, or emphasis, in this statement, Allāh informed Yūsuf that this was undoubtedly going to happen. There were other implications in this prediction that Yūsuf was given. One was that he would not die in the well; two, that he will eventually reunite with his family, and three, at the time of reunion, he will have the upper hand.

---

44 *Yūsuf* (12: 91).
45 *Yūsuf* (12: 97).

This verse also has an optimistic message for the Prophet Muhammad ﷺ during a period of intense difficulty. Through the story of Yūsuf, Allāh reminded him that even though his people had abandoned him, he would eventually become victorious over them. In another sūrah Allāh hinted to the Prophet ﷺ about his migration and triumphant return to Makkah: *'Most certainly, the One Who has ordained the Qur'ān for you will 'ultimately' bring you back home 'to Makkah'.'*[46] Through Sūrah Yūsuf, Allāh reminded the Prophet ﷺ and us that *'surely, with every difficulty comes relief.'*[47]

Knowing how matters will turn out brings us great comfort. Allāh foretold Yūsuf about the end of his life in this world, and He only gives this knowledge to a prophet. As Muslims, we believe in Allāh's cardinal rule that the righteous will inherit Paradise. No matter what is happening in the world, how tough life is, or what difficulties or problems we face, we should always remind ourselves of the ultimate reward: *Jannah,* and that should help us get through.

We notice that in the above verse, Allāh sent Yūsuf a revelation (*waḥy)* even though he was still a child. Some scholars believe that this happened when Yūsuf had become a prophet. However, the majority opinion holds that indeed Yūsuf received this *waḥy* when he was a child, but it was different from the *waḥy* Allāh sends to prophets. Because he was a child, Yūsuf could not be appointed a prophet. There are three different types of *waḥy* mentioned in the Qur'ān. First, the *waḥy* that Allāh sent to non-humans, for example, *'And your Lord inspired the bees: "Make 'your' homes*

46 *al-Qaṣaṣ* (28: 85).
47 *al-Sharḥ* (94:5).

in the mountains, the trees, and in what people construct."'[48] Second, there is a *waḥy* that Allāh sent to his prophets '*...by sending a messenger-angel to reveal whatever He wills by His permission.*'[49] Third, there is a type of *waḥy* one level below what the prophets receive, and it is called *ilhām*. An *ilhām* means an inner voice or thought that comes to someone, and they know it is from Allāh. The most famous case of *ilhām* in the Qur'ān is that of the mother of Mūsā. Allāh says, '*We inspired the mother of Mūsā: "Nurse him, but when you fear for him, put him then into the river, and do not fear or grieve..."*'[50] Possibly, it was an *ilhām* that Yūsuf received while he was in the well. As the well's darkness frightened Yūsuf, Allāh's light and inspiration enveloped him, and he felt reassured.

وَجَآءُوٓ أَبَاهُمۡ عِشَآءٗ يَبۡكُونَ ١٦

Then they returned to their father in the evening, weeping.

The brothers were not supposed to stay out late, but they came back to their father after sunset. They purposely delayed their return to add credibility to their plot. They pretended that they were searching for Yūsuf and did not know what to do. ***'...they returned to their father in the evening, weeping.'*** The brothers' tears were fake, but they

[48] *an-Naḥl* (16: 68).
[49] *ash-Shūrā* (42: 51).
[50] *al-Qaṣaṣ* (28: 7).

needed something to create drama and make their story appear credible to Yāqūb.

Of course, tears do not necessarily establish victimhood as every parent knows! Let us mention a well-known incident from the life of Shurayḥ al-Qāḍī (d. 697), one of the most famous judges in early Islamic history. He was from the generation after the *Ṣaḥābah,* and there are many stories narrated about his life. Once a woman came to Shurayḥ crying hysterically, complaining about an accusation against her. Shurayḥ sat emotionless despite the woman's frantic cries. Even his students were embarrassed and ashamed at what they felt was their teacher's apathy. When the woman left, they asked, 'O Shaykh, why did you not show her some sympathy? She was sobbing and weeping. Maybe some wrong was done to her.' Shurayḥ replied, 'The brothers of Yūsuf were also sobbing and weeping, but they were the ones who had committed the wrong. We base our ruling on facts and not on emotion.' Later, it was in fact discovered that the woman in this case was indeed guilty.

قَالُوا۟ يَـٰٓأَبَانَآ إِنَّا ذَهَبْنَا نَسْتَبِقُ وَتَرَكْنَا يُوسُفَ عِندَ مَتَـٰعِنَا
فَأَكَلَهُ ٱلذِّئْبُ ۖ وَمَآ أَنتَ بِمُؤْمِنٍ لَّنَا وَلَوْ كُنَّا صَـٰدِقِينَ ﴿١٧﴾

They cried, "Our father! We went racing and left Yūsuf with our belongings, and a wolf devoured him! But you will not believe us, no matter how truthful we are."

The brothers, who had rehearsed their story, said, ***'…We went racing and left Yūsuf with our belongings, and a wolf devoured him!'*** Sadly, they had used Yaʿqūb's apprehensions against him in concocting the story of Yūsuf's disappearance. They said they had left Yūsuf to watch their belongings while they raced each other, and then a wolf came and attacked him. The story sounded a bit far-fetched even to them, so they added, ***'…But you will not believe us, no matter how truthful we are.'*** They acknowledged to their father that the version of events might sound preposterous to him but insisted they were nothing but truthful. Sometimes, when we hear something unbelievable, we don't know whether to laugh or cry: this was one of those moments.

وَجَآءُو عَلَىٰ قَمِيصِهِۦ بِدَمٍ كَذِبٍۚ قَالَ بَلْ سَوَّلَتْ لَكُمْ أَنفُسُكُمْ
أَمْرًاۖ فَصَبْرٌ جَمِيلٌۖ وَٱللَّهُ ٱلْمُسْتَعَانُ عَلَىٰ مَا تَصِفُونَ ١٨

And they brought his shirt, stained with false blood. He responded, "No! Your souls must have tempted you to do something 'evil'. So 'I can only endure with' beautiful patience! It is Allāh's help that I seek to bear your claims."

The brothers knew that Yaʿqūb would not believe their story, so they prepared evidence to support their claim, ***'…they brought his shirt, stained with false blood…'*** There is very beautiful Arabic *balāghah* here: the literal translation is 'a lying blood'. Blood doesn't lie, but Allāh ascribed lying to the blood to show it was false blood. They brought forth Yūsuf's blood-stained shirt, but it was not his blood.

In his horror, Yaʿqūb cried out, ***'...No!...'*** In the Arabic language, *bal* translated here as 'no,' is *ḥarf al-iḍrāb*, meaning a thing that completely negates everything that came before it. The Qur'ān used this term to indicate that the brothers' claim was a blatant lie, and the truth was to follow. Yaʿqūb did not believe them, so he said, ***'...Your souls must have tempted you...'*** Since Yaʿqūb's intuition informed him about the plot, but he did not know the full story, he left the matter open. Through Allāh, he had inner certitude that Yūsuf wasn't dead.

When Yūsuf had first told him the dream, Yaʿqūb had warned him not to inform his brothers about it lest they devise a plot against him. Alas! What he feared had come true. Yaʿqūb understood that the brothers had concocted a scheme, but he appealed to their conscience to rectify the wrong. That is why he did not outright tell them, 'You have done wrong,' but rather, *'Your souls must have tempted you.'* He treated them with a bit of psychoanalysis, saying, 'How in good conscience could you have done this?' Instead of criticizing the action, he criticized the intention and psychology behind it, indirectly calling it a plot of *Shayṭān*.

Yaʿqūb turned away in grief, saying, ***"...'I can only endure with' beautiful patience!"*** Patience entails restraining oneself, even when the pain is acute. The reason why it is so difficult is that it requires us to control in the face of an overpowering urge to act. Our blood pressure soars, and we want to scream and cry, yet we exhibit grace and dignity amid grief. Our Prophet ﷺ told us that, 'The strong are not the best wrestlers. Verily, the strong are only those who control themselves when they are angry.'[51]

Patience is of three types: patience in the face of calamities, patience in withholding from sins, and patience in persistence in performing acts of worship. Patience also has levels: a person may be patient fleetingly, another may be steadfastly patient, and yet another could be patient to the level of excellence. The trial of losing a child requires the most excellent type of patience, as no parent wants their child to die while they live. When faced with the extreme loss, Yaʿqūb said he would observe *'ṣabrun jamīl'*, or a 'beautiful patience'. The scholars say that 'beautiful patience' is one in which one does not seek people's sympathy and takes his grief directly to Allāh. Yaʿqūb embodied this quality, as later in this sūrah we will hear him say, *'I complain of my anguish and sorrow only to Allāh.'*[52]

The Qur'ān says, *'Allāh is truly with those who are patient'*.[53] There are only a handful of nouns that Allāh uses to describe the characteristics of people who He is 'with'. Of them are *al-muttaqīn* (the God-conscious, pious); *al-sādiqīn* (the truthful, sincere), and *al-sabirīn* (those who are patient). Allāh says that He shall reward the patient *bi ghayri hisāb* (without measure or limit). Without a doubt, those who observe 'beautiful patience' Allāh will grant them this ultimate reward.

Yaʿqūb then said, ***'...It is Allāh's help that I seek...'*** This phrase, *wa-Allāhu al-Mustaʿān*, is one we should memorize

---

51 *Ṣaḥīḥ* of al-Bukhārī (5763).

52 *Yūsuf* (12: 86).

53 *al-Baqarah* (2: 153).

and use frequently. Yaʿqūb felt helpless, so he sought help from Allāh to deal with his grief. Allāh says in the Qur'ān, *'And whoever puts their trust in Allāh, then He 'alone' is sufficient for them.'*[54] It shows us that the believer is never alone or without assistance because Allāh is with them.

وَجَآءَتْ سَيَّارَةٌ فَأَرْسَلُوا۟ وَارِدَهُمْ فَأَدْلَىٰ دَلْوَهُۥ ۖ قَالَ يَٰبُشْرَىٰ هَٰذَا
غُلَٰمٌ ۚ وَأَسَرُّوهُ بِضَٰعَةً ۚ وَٱللَّهُ عَلِيمٌۢ بِمَا يَعْمَلُونَ ﴿١٩﴾

And there came some travellers, and they sent their water-boy who let down his bucket into the well. He cried out, "Oh, what a great find! Here is a boy!" And they took him secretly 'to be sold' as merchandise, but Allāh is All-Knowing of what they did.

Eventually, ***'...there came some travellers...'*** to gather water from the well. *Sayyārah,* translated here as 'travellers,' comes from *yasīru* and refers to seasoned travellers, in this case, a caravan. The caravan stopped ***'...and they sent their water-boy who let down his bucket into the well...'*** There was one person assigned to collect the water, and he lowered his bucket. The fact that he had to lower his own bucket shows us that Yūsuf was in a very primitive well. An oft-frequented well, generally, has a pulley and bucket attached to it.

[54] *al-Ṭalāq* (65: 3).

When the bucket came back up, the water-drawer exclaimed, ***'Oh, what a great find! Here is a boy!'*** Why was he so happy? Because this is the era of slavery, and one of the most precious, prized, and expensive commodities was a slave. The people of the caravan had no intention to find the boy's parents and return him home. Instead, they decided to sell him into slavery. ***'...And they took him secretly 'to be sold' as merchandise...'*** It means they hid Yūsuf surreptitiously in their belongings, knowing their actions to be wrong. The Qur'ān says, ***'...but Allāh is All-Knowing of what they did.'***

Thus, the caravan clandestinely transported Yūsuf from Palestine to Egypt, hidden amongst the sacks of merchandise.

وَشَرَوْهُ بِثَمَنٍۭ بَخْسٍ دَرَٰهِمَ مَعْدُودَةٍ وَكَانُوا۟ فِيهِ مِنَ ٱلزَّٰهِدِينَ ﴿٢٠﴾

They 'later' sold him for a cheap price, just a few silver coins, only wanting to get rid of him.

The caravan sold Yūsuf for less than what he was worth. They got ***'...a cheap price...'*** The word *bakhs* here means they suffered a loss in the trade, which we may interpret in two ways. Firstly, that Yūsuf was invaluable, and no matter what price they had sold him for, it would never have been enough. Secondly, they sold Yūsuf for far less than they would sell an average slave. If the market value was several hundred silver coins, they sold him for a fraction of that.

Ibn Abbās said maybe a tenth of his worth. To emphasize the point, Allāh says, ***'...just a few silver coins...'*** The fact that you could count them shows how low an amount they got from selling Yūsuf.

The word translated as coins here is *darāhim,* which is the plural of a *dirham*. The word comes from the ancient Greek *drachm* because Greeks were the first people to use it. The Romans minted their own gold coins and called them a *denarius*. At the time of the Prophet ﷺ, the Arabs did not have their own currency, so they used the Roman and Persian coins. The early Umayyad *khalīfah*, 'Abdul Malik ibn Marwān was the first to mint gold and silver for the Muslims, and he called the silver coin *dirham* and the gold coin *dīnār*. The words used to denote these ancient currencies have survived to this day. (The dirham is the official currency of the UAE, while the dinar is the monetary unit in Algeria, Bahrain, Iraq, Jordan, Kuwait, Libya, and Tunisia.)

The fact that they sold Yūsuf for a paltry sum shows that they considered him insignificant and ***'...only wanting to get rid of him...'*** Had they sold Yūsuf in a legal market, he would have fetched a fortune, because the most expensive type of slave is a young boy who could serve for years on end. But because they didn't have to pay for him, the low sale price was of no consequence to them. It is human psychology that when we get something for free, we do not value it. An example of this in our times is our religion, Islam. Those born Muslim typically don't appreciate the faith like the converts to Islam do. The converts had to find Islam through research and sacrifice, and sometimes by damaging their ties with non-Muslim relatives. Allāh says the caravan didn't consider Yūsuf to be significant because he was stolen merchandise, and they wanted to dispose of him quickly. When people sell stolen goods, they do it quickly before getting caught. The travellers felt guilty because they had captured an innocent boy who didn't deserve capture.

وَقَالَ ٱلَّذِى ٱشْتَرَىٰهُ مِن مِّصْرَ لِٱمْرَأَتِهِۦٓ أَكْرِمِى مَثْوَىٰهُ عَسَىٰٓ
أَن يَنفَعَنَآ أَوْ نَتَّخِذَهُۥ وَلَدًاۚ وَكَذَٰلِكَ مَكَّنَّا لِيُوسُفَ فِى ٱلْأَرْضِ
وَلِنُعَلِّمَهُۥ مِن تَأْوِيلِ ٱلْأَحَادِيثِۚ وَٱللَّهُ غَالِبٌ عَلَىٰٓ أَمْرِهِۦ
وَلَٰكِنَّ أَكْثَرَ ٱلنَّاسِ لَا يَعْلَمُونَ ﴿٢١﴾

The man from Egypt who bought him said to his wife, "Take good care of him, perhaps he may be useful to us, or we may adopt him as a son." This is how We established Yūsuf in the land, so that We might teach him the interpretation of dreams. Allāh's Will always prevails, but most people do not know.

The caravan took Yūsuf over the Sinai Peninsula into the land of Egypt. The Qur'ān calls ***'The man from Egypt who bought him...'*** Al-ʿAzīz, which simply means an honourable man. It is interesting to note that later in the story, Yūsuf calls himself Al-ʿAzīz. Because of this, several

Muslim scholars have said that Yūsuf's master was the minister of finance, like what Yūsuf became some years later. There is an indication that Yūsuf eventually took on the role of his master, who was a noble minister, one level below the king.

Al-ʿAzīz said to his wife, ***'...Take good care of him...'*** In other words, treat him nicely and give him all that he needs; make his accommodation comfortable. The minister sensed that Yūsuf was not an ordinary boy, so he instructed his wife to treat him honourably and not like the other slaves. Why? Because ***'...he may be useful to us, or we may adopt him as a son.'*** Some early scholars, such as Ibn Masʿūd, said that three people showed the depth of *firāsah,* or intuition, when judging a person and their character. The first was Al-ʿAzīz when he saw Yūsuf. The second was the daughter of the shepherd in the story of Mūsa when she told her father, *'...Hire him* (meaning Mūsa). *The best man for employment is definitely the strong and trustworthy 'one'.'*[55] The third was Abū Bakr as-Ṣiddīq, when, on his deathbed, he chose ʿUmar to lead the *khilāfah* after him.

'...This is how We established Yūsuf in the land...' If Allāh had willed, Yūsuf could have ended up in a horrible situation with a cruel master, but He had a better plan for him. Allāh lifted Yūsuf from the depths of a remote well and placed him into the home of a high-ranking Egyptian minister only to eventually make him the minister of finance. All along, Allāh was in control of Yūsuf's affairs,

---

[55] *al-Qaṣaṣ* (28: 26).

and nothing could have frustrated the Will of Allāh, as we shall see.

Allāh says that He planned this *'...so that We might teach him the interpretation of dreams...'* We shall see this beautiful phrase repeated in two other verses in this sūrah. Dream interpretation is one of the few sciences that Allāh blesses a person innately; it is not something one can learn from a book. All prophets of Allāh knew this science, including the Prophet Muḥammad ﷺ, but especially the Prophet Yūsuf. In this verse, it seems as if Allāh is saying, 'Yūsuf will interpret the dreams of others, including the King, but all of this will be to fulfill his first dream about the sun, the moon, and the stars prostrating to him.'

What happened to Yūsuf and the sequence in which it occurred was not by chance, but rather Allāh had predestined it. It was a Divine Plan. The brothers committed a crime, which triggered Yūsuf's journey from the deserts of Palestine to the heart of one of the most powerful kingdoms of the ancient world: Egypt. ***'... Allāh's Will always prevails, but most people do not know.'*** This verse reminds us of a quintessential aspect of our creed: *tawakkul* or trust in Allāh. It means that everything happens according to Allāh's plan. While we must do our part to guard against evil, as did Yāqūb, we should know that the outcome rests with Allāh, that it is His Plan that prevails, and that He is the best planner. If we truly understand that nothing happens except what Allāh has willed, we will put our trust in Him Alone and accept

His Decree, but, as the verse says, '***most people do not understand.***'

وَلَمَّا بَلَغَ أَشُدَّهُۥٓ ءَاتَيۡنَٰهُ حُكۡمٗا وَعِلۡمٗاۚ وَكَذَٰلِكَ
نَجۡزِي ٱلۡمُحۡسِنِينَ ٢٢

And when he reached maturity, We gave him wisdom and knowledge. This is how We reward the doers of good.

Brevity is the hallmark of the Qur'ān. In these few words, the Qur'ān moves from Yūsuf's childhood and heralds his entering manhood. Yūsuf had now '***...reached maturity,...***' and with its onset, Allāh had given him 'wisdom and knowledge'. Arab linguists say that the term *ashudd* applies to the age between 18 and 40 years. After 40 years, one begins old age or *shaykhūkha*. Some scholars say that Yūsuf was 30 years old at this time, but most say he had just reached the age of manhood, perhaps around 19 or 20 years of age.

'***...We gave him wisdom and knowledge...***' *Ḥukm* in this verse means 'wisdom', but there is another meaning of it, and that is 'power'. Allāh combines both of these meanings here because one without the other is incomplete; put together, they equal perfection. Although Yūsuf had no power at this moment, the verse implies that he shall attain it while still a young man. *'Ilm* means 'knowledge'. One may possess the knowledge, yet not know how to act upon it. *Ḥikmah* means that someone has the knowledge and knows how to use it wisely. Hence Allāh's statement: 'We gave Yūsuf both *'ilm* and *ḥukm*.' These qualities reached perfection when Allāh conferred prophethood upon Yūsuf.

'...This is how We reward the doers of good.' Let's take a moment to reflect on this statement. Allāh is saying, 'We gave Yūsuf wisdom and knowledge, and this is how We reward the *muḥsinīn,* the doers of good.' When we strive to be righteous, Allāh will reward us with wisdom and knowledge. If we have the *taqwā* of Allāh, He will give us wisdom, power and knowledge. Yūsuf will need all these qualities to face the challenges that lay ahead.

PART THREE

The Seduction

وَرَٰوَدَتۡهُ ٱلَّتِي هُوَ فِي بَيۡتِهَا عَن نَّفۡسِهِۦ وَغَلَّقَتِ ٱلۡأَبۡوَٰبَ
وَقَالَتۡ هَيۡتَ لَكَۚ قَالَ مَعَاذَ ٱللَّهِۖ إِنَّهُۥ رَبِّيٓ أَحۡسَنَ مَثۡوَايَۖ
إِنَّهُۥ لَا يُفۡلِحُ ٱلظَّٰلِمُونَ ﴿٢٣﴾

And the lady, in whose house he lived, tried to seduce him. She locked the doors 'firmly' and said, "Come to me!" He replied, "Allāh is my refuge! It is 'not right to betray' my Master, who has taken good care of me. Indeed, the wrongdoers never succeed."

The Prophet ﷺ told us, that on his Ascension (*al-Mi'rāj)* "I saw Yūsuf, who was given half of (this world's) beauty"[56] Imagine, Yūsuf alone had half the beauty of every handsome and beautiful person from the beginning of time until the Day of Judgement!

The effect of Yūsuf's unparalleled beauty was such that as he grew into manhood, ***'...the lady, in whose house he lived, tried to seduce him...'*** *Rāwadah* means 'to seduce or to entice,' and the verb here indicates that she did it repeatedly. In other words, this was not just a one-off event. As Yūsuf matured, these incidents intensified. Allāh does not say, 'the wife of Al-'Azīz tried to seduce him,' He says the seductress was *'...the lady, in whose house he lived...'* to emphasize how difficult it must have been for Yūsuf. He lived in her house, as her and her husband's servant, giving

56 *Ṣaḥīḥ* of Muslim (162).

her authority over him. Allāh tells us it was no ordinary seduction. It wasn't just a woman trying to seduce a man. Yūsuf was her slave, and slaves don't have rights (especially at that time and place). She, on the other hand, was a free person from the elite of society. As if this wasn't difficult enough, Yūsuf had just reached manhood, and a young man at the prime of his youth has the least self-control. The enticement of Al-ʿAzīz's wife had increased over time, and given Yūsuf's low position in the house, warding her off was becoming ever more difficult. Yūsuf must have felt that he had no escape from sexual harassment.

"...She locked the doors 'firmly'..." There is a *shaddah* in the verb 'to close' (*viz., 'ghallaqa'*) for emphasis, indicating that she did not just close the doors, but she locked them and then double locked them. She made an extra effort to bolt not only one entry but all the doors. The beauty of the Qur'ān is that Allāh does not go into details when there is no need. She locked all the doors; the rest we can understand. She had been planning for this moment, and finally, it had arrived. Perhaps her husband was away for an extended period, or this was the time when there were no other servants in the house.

Our Prophet ﷺ told us, 'No man is alone with a woman, but the *Shayṭān* is the third one present.'[57] And we can see from this example why *Shayṭān* invites himself when two persons of the opposite gender are alone. In the present case, the two were not only alone; with the doors locked, there was no possibility of interruption. The

---

[57] *Sunan* al-Tirmidhī (2165).

woman had beautified herself and made sure Yūsuf knew her intention, to such an extent that Ibn Abbās said that she was lying down seductively, waiting for him.

She said, *'hayta lak'*, meaning, ***'Come to me!'*** Scholars of the Arabic language have tried to explain *hayta,* a word not commonly used. The reason Allāh used an obscure word, it seems, was to show that she was using a seductive, vulgar language. There might not even be an Arabic equivalent, so Allāh used an uncommon common. In simple terms, she was saying coyly, 'Come on! Let's do it.' She used a crude expression to put her message across.

Immediately, Yūsuf said: *maʿādha Allāh,* ***'Allāh is my refuge!'*** There is so much eloquence in this phrase. Yūsuf could have said *aʿūdhu billāh,* meaning 'I seek refuge in Allāh,' but instead, he said *maʿādha Allāh,* meaning, 'The One whose refuge I seek is Allāh.' What he meant is that it is always Allāh Alone Whose help and protection we should seek; that Allāh is the perfect Protector, even when we sometimes forget to beseech His protection.

Then, ***"...It is 'not right to betray' my Master, who has taken good care of me..."*** There are two opinions about this phrase: did he mean 'my master' as in the husband of the lady, or did he mean 'my Master' as in my Lord and Creator, Allāh? Many scholars understand this phrase to mean, 'your husband is my master, and he has made my life comfortable.' But Yūsuf's statement that ***'Allāh is my refuge'*** indicates that he meant 'Allāh is my Master,' not Al-ʿAzīz. The word *Rabb* can mean both 'Lord' and 'Master'. It is interesting to note that many interpreters of the Qur'ān suggest the latter, meaning that the reference is to his master and the husband of the temptress. Allāh knows best, but it makes more sense because he was talking about Allāh. He was a prophet after all; what difference would it make how the husband treated him, the action of fornication would not have been justified either way? Moreover, what the woman had invited him to was a crime in Yūsuf's religion. What proves this point is the ending of the verse. *'... **Indeed, the wrongdoers never succeed.**'* In this statement, Yūsuf was alluding to Allāh and not the husband. Since the beginning and the end of the verse point to Allāh, it is logical that the middle also meant Allāh.

The instantaneous response of Yūsuf, when faced with the trial of temptation, was to turn to Allāh, something all Muslims should do when tempted by sin. We will never be able to overcome evil by ourselves because we do not have the strength to fight on our own. We need Allāh to protect us in a moment of weakness. He is the Only One who will give us the strength to fight off temptation. Allāh says in the Qur'ān, *'And if you are tempted by Shayṭān, then seek refuge with Allāh. Indeed, He 'alone' is the All-Hearing, All-Knowing.'*[58]

وَلَقَدْ هَمَّتْ بِهِۦ ۖ وَهَمَّ بِهَا لَوْلَآ أَن رَّءَا بُرْهَٰنَ رَبِّهِۦ ۚ كَذَٰلِكَ لِنَصْرِفَ
عَنْهُ ٱلسُّوٓءَ وَٱلْفَحْشَآءَ ۚ إِنَّهُۥ مِنْ عِبَادِنَا ٱلْمُخْلَصِينَ ﴿٢٤﴾

Indeed, she did desire him, and he desired her, had he not seen a sign from his Lord. This is how We kept evil and indecency

58 *al-Fuṣṣilat* (41: 36).

away from him, for he was truly one of Our chosen servants.

This verse is perhaps the most commented on in the sūrah, and the classical scholars have differed over its meaning– ***'Indeed, she did desire him, and he desired her, had he not seen a sign from His Lord...'*** Why is this problematic? Many medieval and some modern scholars found this problematic because they questioned how a prophet of Allāh could desire her, meaning want to commit an illicit act? They said this could not be possible, and they understood the verse thus: 'She desired him, and he *would have* desired her *had he not* seen the evidence from Allāh.' So, this means he did not have the *hamm*, or strong desire for her. On the contrary, the woman had a burning desire to act on her passion and had planned to pursue it aggressively.

Hence, the predominant interpretation is that Yūsuf did not have any desire because a prophet could not desire a woman who was not lawful for him. They say he was too righteous, scrupulous, and noble to have a desire of this kind. However, another group of scholars (and in this case they are a minority) did not see a problem if Yūsuf did feel a desire for her, because *hamm* is a desire without action, and what is sinful is the *action*, not the *desire*. They contend that Yūsuf's possible inclination toward her did not belittle his rank; if anything, it showed his humanity, and Yūsuf deserves praise because he restrained himself from committing a major sin in the face of a well-planned enticement by a charming woman. The Prophet ﷺ told us that if someone '...intended to perform an evil deed, but did not do it, then Allāh writes it down with Himself as a complete good deed.'[59]

Given the preceding discussion, we may ask: Can the prophets of Allāh make mistakes or commit sins? Again, scholars have different opinions. The strongest among them is that the prophets of Allāh are protected from major sins, as well as from acts that would cast doubt on their noble character, such as lying or cheating. It is, however, possible for the prophets of Allāh to make mistakes arising from human emotions, such as anger, or acting on a desire that, although permissible, would lead to the displeasure of Allāh. For example, our father Ādam wanted eternal life, so he ate from the forbidden tree. Prophets can be overcome with natural desire or emotion, but they would not act upon an indecent thought because Allāh protects them from such action. They can impulsively act on a feeling once, but any time a prophet does so, Allāh immediately corrects him, and he stops. The prophets do not commit repetitive sins, but they may commit isolated minor sins.

Therefore, there is nothing wrong with taking the verse at face value, and our respect and honour for Yūsuf only increases. Of course he desired her – any man in a similar situation would! But as a true believer, he controlled his desire and didn't act upon it. Why?

The Qur'ān says ***'...had he not seen a sign from his Lord...'*** *Burhān,* translated here as a 'sign' means a clear proof. What *burhān* did Yūsuf see? There are seven or eight different opinions, but the strongest seems to be that the

---

[59] *Ṣaḥīḥ* of Muslim (235).

sign that Allāh gave Yūsuf was his knowledge that Allāh was watching him. In Arabic, the word for absolute proof is *burhān,* and Yūsuf had the certainty that Allāh was watching him. ***'...This is how We kept evil and indecency away from him...'*** The word *sū* is any type of evil, and *faḥshā'* is evil of a sexual nature. By using two different terms, Allāh exonerates the character of Yūsuf: he never committed any evil deed. So the verse informs us that the knowledge and certainty that Yūsuf had diverted him away from committing the lewd act.

'...for he was truly one of Our chosen servants.' There are two ways of reciting this verse. The Qur'ān has many recitations or *qirā'āt,* and they are all considered equally as Divine Revelations. The majority of Muslims recite the Qur'ān according to the *riwāyah* of *Ḥafs 'an 'Asim,* but other places in the Muslim world have other recitations with minor differences in the tenses and pronunciation. In some *qirā'āt,* this verse is pronounced as *mukhlaṣīn,* meaning 'chosen purified servant', wherase others recite *mukhliṣīn* meaning 'sincere servant'. The first word means 'Yūsuf was of Our servants whom We chose,' whereas the second word would translate as 'Yūsuf was of our servants who had sincerity.' Both of these are accurate and authentic. Yūsuf had sincerity, and Allāh chose him. The way to become Allāh's chosen is to be sincere. This profound verse means that if we are sincere and truthful to Allāh, He will avert evil from us.

The desire for an illegal or illicit thing is one of the most challenging temptations. In our times, we face these challenges on an almost daily basis. That is why our

Prophet ﷺ said, 'There are seven whom Allāh will shade with His Shade on the Day when there will be no shade except His.' Who are they? The hadith tells us that one of them is: 'A man who is called by a woman of rank and beauty and said, "I fear Allāh."'[60] In the example of Yūsuf, we see this category personified. Through sincerity, we can resist temptation and earn a place under Allāh's Shade.

وَٱسْتَبَقَا ٱلْبَابَ وَقَدَّتْ قَمِيصَهُۥ مِن دُبُرٍ وَأَلْفَيَا سَيِّدَهَا لَدَا ٱلْبَابِ ۚ قَالَتْ مَا جَزَآءُ مَنْ أَرَادَ بِأَهْلِكَ سُوٓءًا إِلَّآ أَن يُسْجَنَ أَوْ عَذَابٌ أَلِيمٌ ﴿٢٥﴾

They raced for the door and she tore his shirt from the back, only to find her husband at the door. She cried, "What is the penalty for someone who intended evil for your wife, except for imprisonment or a painful punishment?"

After Yūsuf refused her overtures, he turned to leave as quickly as he could. ***'They raced for the door...'*** In these few words, Allāh gives us the whole picture. There were two people in a locked room, and both sprinted towards the door—Yūsuf, to escape the call to evil, and the wife of Al-ʿAzīz, to stop him from leaving. Their outward actions

---

60 *Ṣaḥīḥ* of al-Bukhārī (620).

appeared the same, but their spiritual and emotional intentions were opposite; Yūsuf wanted to evade sin, and the wife of Al-ʿAzīz desired to commit it. Don't judge a person by an outward deed until you are aware of their intentions!

'...she tore his shirt from the back ...' In the process of trying to prevent Yūsuf from leaving, the wife of Al-ʿAzīz tore his shirt. In her zealousness and crazed state, she held onto Yūsuf's shirt and was physically pulling him and begging him to come back. In his earnestness to leave, Yūsuf struggled and had his shirt torn.

'...only to find her husband at the door...' The word *alfayā* implies that they did not expect to find the husband at the door. The wife had planned to commit the indecent act at a time when no one was home or expected to return. To be on the safe side, she had also locked all the doors. Now she was shocked to find her husband at the door. Clearly, he wasn't supposed to be there!

Notice the beauty of the eloquence of the Qur'ān here. The word used for her husband is *sayyidaha*, meaning 'her master'. It would seem more appropriate to say, 'his master', meaning Yūsuf's master, or 'her husband'. But Allāh, in His eloquent accuracy, merges the two and says, 'they found her master at the door'. The profundity here is to show us how depraved this woman had become. She had betrayed the trust of her husband, whom she should have given her respect and obedience. By calling her husband 'her master', Allāh emphasized what an evil act of betrayal she had committed.

'...She cried, "What is the penalty for someone who intended evil for your wife..."' This verse proves that she was not just someone overcome by lust, but that she was also cunning. Within a heartbeat, she invented a lie. Another person caught in this act might have been speechless and ashamed, but she instantly found a way out: blame Yūsuf. But she didn't say, 'he who tried to rape me,' but 'he who intended evil'. She could not accuse Yūsuf of committing the act, so she accused him of having intended it. She did this for two reasons. Firstly, nothing had happened. Secondly, if she said that something had happened, then the burden of proof would be higher, and she would also be in trouble if she didn't provide any evidence.

It is a standard tactic of evildoers and criminals to lay the blame at the victim's door, which is worse than the crime itself. Allāh says, *'And whoever commits an evil or sinful deed then blames it on an innocent person, they will definitely bear the guilt of slander and blatant sin.'*[61] Those who commit sins end up committing more sins to cover them up, as we learned from the brothers of Yūsuf. The wife of Al-ʿAzīz planned to commit one sin, and that led her down a slippery slope of many more sins. Every sin creates a domino effect. The most famous example of such behavior is Iblīs. When he refused to prostrate to Ādam, he committed a cardinal sin, but he doubled down, and accused Allāh of, *'...leaving me to stray...'*[62] So, we see that blaming others for one's own sin is a Satanic trait.

---

61 *an-Nisā'* (4: 112).
62 *al-Aʿrāf* (7: 16).

The wife of the Al-ʿAzīz suggested punishment for Yūsuf to deflect blame from herself. She said Yūsuf deserved nothing ***'...except for imprisonment or a painful punishment?'***

قَالَ هِىَ رَٰوَدَتْنِى عَن نَّفْسِى ۚ وَشَهِدَ شَاهِدٌ مِّنْ أَهْلِهَآ إِن كَانَ
قَمِيصُهُۥ قُدَّ مِن قُبُلٍ فَصَدَقَتْ وَهُوَ مِنَ ٱلْكَٰذِبِينَ ﴿٢٦﴾

Yūsuf responded, "It was she who tried to seduce me." And a witness from her own family testified: "If his shirt is torn from the front, then she has told the truth, and he is a liar.

Yūsuf immediately defended himself by saying, ***'It was she who tried to seduce me.'*** He did not allow the accusation to go unchallenged. Protecting one's honour is the right thing to do, except in situations where expediency dictates silence, as we will see that another time when Yūsuf was accused of a crime, he remained silent. It is not obligatory to defend one's honour against every accusation.

Yūsuf had pushed back on slander when he was a slave but did not respond to an accusation when he was a minister. The first time he defended himself because a slave accused of a crime could easily land in jail. At the time of the second accusation, he was a minister and faced no threat of imprisonment or physical harm. At the second incident, responding would have led to the discovery of his identity, and that would have been problematic. Yūsuf looked at the bigger picture and analyzed the consequences of his actions. Sometimes, allegations are not against us but our religion. Should we, therefore, respond to every attack against Islam? The answer is that sometimes it is obligatory to rebut, especially when we are weak and humiliated, and at other times, when Islam is strong, we do not need to worry about the accusation because it will not harm us.

In this case, Yūsuf responded by saying, *'It was she who tried to seduce me.'* His statement was not vague like hers. Generally speaking, the one who makes a specific accusation is more truthful than the one whose charge is vague. Similarly, the guilty one often responds to an allegation with, 'Nothing happened,' or 'I don't know what he is talking about.' Notice that Yūsuf did not accuse her in the first person; instead, he spoke indirectly, even though she was standing in front of him. Some scholars have inferred from this that Yūsuf did not accuse her directly to show her respect, even though he knew she was blameworthy. So he appealed to the husband as if she was not present.

Al-ʿAzīz had a difficult case on his hand. On the one side was his wife, and on the other a slave. While he was pondering how to establish the truth, a witness from the family spoke.

Allāh says, ***'…And a witness from her own family…'*** *Shāhid* means somebody who saw. Allāh used the word *shāhid*, yet this man was not a witness to the actual event.

Why does Allāh call him a *shāhid* when he was not a physical witness? Some scholars have said that Allāh called him a *shāhid,* because Allāh was the witness, and what the man said was the truth. Others noted that Allāh called him a witness because he cited a universal rule (i.e., examine the evidence!) which was equally applicable here, regardless of who was right or wrong. It is also possible that this person had witnessed the overall conduct of the wife towards Yūsuf and knew that she was trying to seduce him. Generally, when one is overcome with lust and emotion, it is difficult to completely hide that emotion.

So who was this *shāhid*? The exegetes have several opinions, and the most sound is that it was a cousin or relative of hers who lived in the house. We know that it was a relative because Allāh says *min ahlihā* meaning 'from her family'. It seems Allāh mentioned this, so everyone knew this person was related to Al-ʿAzīz's wife and could not be biased against her. Generally speaking, people of the same family stick together and help each other out. Allāh said that this witness was a man from her own family, so he was not someone trying to settle a grudge. He was not a slave (for there might be a grude that would make such a person lie); he was a free man from her own family. He made a fair statement, and it seems he wanted the truth to come out. The witness said, ***'...If his shirt is torn from the front, then she has told the truth, and he is a liar.'*** It is so because if Yūsuf had tried to assault the woman and she defended herself, in the resulting scuffle, his shirt would have been torn from the front.

وَإِن كَانَ قَمِيصُهُۥ قُدَّ مِن دُبُرٍ فَكَذَبَتْ وَهُوَ مِنَ ٱلصَّٰدِقِينَ ﴿٢٧﴾

"But if it is torn from the back, then she has lied, and he is truthful."

Conversely, if the opposite is the case, ***'…then she has lied, and he is truthful.'*** A shirt torn from the back would prove that Yūsuf was running away, and she was trying to stop him. So, where the shirt was torn from provided an important clue. In Islamic law, it is permissible to base a judgement on circumstantial evidence. It is a controversial point, and we won't go into too much detail of *fiqh*, but most scholars in our history have said that to prosecute any crime, there must be two adult witnesses (except for the case of *zinā'*, or adultery, which requires four). According to that understanding, fingerprints or video testimonials (as modern examples) would not be considered as decisive evidence in a court of law. There were a few scholars, among them Ibn Taymiyyah and Ibn Al-Qayyim, who argued that the testimony of two witnesses was not necessary if there was enough circumstantial evidence to show that a crime had occurred. In our time, many judges in the Muslim world argue that evidence like DNA and fingerprints should be allowed to play a role. And this verse plays a role in the debate, because Allāh validated the testimony of a person who was not an eyewitness, showing that circumstantial evidence is admissible.

It is interesting to note here the repeated use of two motifs: racing and shirts. Earlier in the story, the brothers said they were racing when the wolf attacked Yūsuf, and they brought back his shirt as evidence of his death. The scholars say that it was the shirt that alerted Yaʿqūb to the fact that his children were lying, because it was bloodstained but not torn. Here too, we find these motifs of racing and the shirt. This torn shirt now had the power to save Yūsuf's reputation.

فَلَمَّا رَءَا قَمِيصَهُۥ قُدَّ مِن دُبُرٍ قَالَ إِنَّهُۥ مِن كَيْدِكُنَّ إِنَّ
كَيْدَكُنَّ عَظِيمٌ ﴿٢٨﴾

So when her husband saw that Yūsuf's shirt was torn from the back, he said 'to her', "This must be 'an example' of the cunning of you 'women'! Indeed, your cunning is so shrewd!"

Until this point, Al-ʿAzīz was not sure who instigated the encounter, but when he ***'...saw that Yūsuf's shirt was torn from the back...'*** the evidence began to stare him in the face. Now everything fell into place, and he realized that his wife was lying. So, he chastised her, saying, '... ***This must be 'an example' of the cunning of you 'women'! Indeed, your cunning is so shrewd!'***

يُوسُفُ أَعۡرِضۡ عَنۡ هَٰذَاۚ وَٱسۡتَغۡفِرِي لِذَنۢبِكِۖ إِنَّكِ كُنتِ
مِنَ ٱلۡخَاطِـِٔينَ ٢٩

"O Yūsuf! Forget about this. And you 'O wife'! Seek forgiveness for your sin. It certainly has been your fault."

At this moment, there are four people in the room: the wife of Al-ʿAzīz, Yūsuf, Al-ʿAzīz, and the witness. Al-ʿAzīz did not want this matter to go any further. He, of course, would not talk about it, and his wife was too ashamed, and the witness, a relative of hers and trustworthy, could not be expected to tell anyone. That left only Yūsuf, who could divulge the secret, so he turned to him and said, ***'O Yūsuf! Forget about this...'***, meaning, 'Ignore it, don't tell anybody, let's just pretend this never happened.'

'...And you 'O wife'! Seek forgiveness for your sin. It certainly has been your fault.' The question arises, why did he let her off with a slap on the wrist despite the severe offense? What makes the most sense from a human psychology perspective, is that he wanted to keep this affair secret because it would have harmed his reputation. The scholars point out that one of the dangers of ego and pride is that a person tolerates corruption in his household, as long as it stays private. If the news gets out, it will damage the reputation. In our time, the rich and the famous are willing to overlook evil, as long as it doesn't get into the public eye. They will even turn to bribery and corruption to avoid a public scandal. We see the same sentiment reflected thousands of years ago. Al-ʿAzīz was thinking about damage control. He underestimated the extent of his wife's passion for Yūsuf and the danger of the situation. He believed that this was an isolated incident that will never happen again, so he did not remove Yūsuf from the household, nor banish his wife.

One interesting point is that Al-ʿAzīz and his wife were not Muslims, yet he told her to, '*...Seek forgiveness for your sin...*' He wanted her to seek forgiveness from his gods and not from him. He knew that infidelity was a sin, even though he didn't believe in Yūsuf's monotheistic *Sharīʿah*. This notion is so firmly embedded in our *fiṭrah* that even today when vices are so common, extramarital relations are considered wrong. Today, one may do pretty much anything as long as one is not married, but once they are, then infidelity is deemed wrong. By nature, humans abhor cheating on the spouse, and this is what we see reflected in the culture of ancient Egypt.

وَقَالَ نِسْوَةٌ فِي ٱلْمَدِينَةِ ٱمْرَأَتُ ٱلْعَزِيزِ تُرَٰوِدُ فَتَىٰهَا عَن نَّفْسِهِۦ ۖ
قَدْ شَغَفَهَا حُبًّا ۖ إِنَّا لَنَرَىٰهَا فِي ضَلَٰلٍ مُّبِينٍ ﴿٣٠﴾

Some women of the city gossiped, "The Chief Minister's wife is trying to seduce her slave-boy. Love for him has plagued her heart. Indeed, we see that she is clearly mistaken."

Despite the best attempts of Al-ʿAzīz to keep the matter quiet, the news began to spread. It is the *Sunnah* of Allāh that gossip spreads, and as it does, it grows bigger. ***'Some women of the city gossiped, "The Chief Minister's wife is trying to seduce her slave-boy..."'*** How did people find out? Most scholars said that it was from the slaves of the household; they didn't blame any of the four that were in the room. We know that Yūsuf would not have said anything. Al-ʿAzīz himself was too embarrassed, and the wife would have been as well. The 'witness' had protective jealousy for the family, so it wasn't likely to be him. It could also have been that the wife's passion for Yūsuf was so apparent that people had no difficulty noticing. The slaves began to whisper to other slaves, and the news spread until it finally reached the the wives of the nobility. And of course, with gossip, all drama intensifies!

They said, ***'...Love for him has plagued her heart...'*** The scholars said this indicated an intense sexual love. The word *'shaghaf'* refers to the interior of the heart, suggesting that the love had penetrated its depths and reached the core of her soul; she was utterly consumed by it. All other matters and affairs of this world were insignificant in the face of her passion for Yūsuf. As the women gossiped, they stressed that the infatuated lady was a minister's wife and Yūsuf her slave and that it was she who tried to seduce him. They used the word *turāwidu* when referring to her attempts to seduce him, implying that she had not been successful, which only added to her humiliation. They described her as being so overcome by her lust, that she didn't care that it was gravely wrong. ***'...Indeed, we see that she is clearly mistaken.'*** From this, we can see that her reputation was in tatters.

Islam puts gossip under different categories. One of the most common is *ghībah*, or back-biting, which has been defined as 'speaking about another person, in their absence, in a manner that they would not like, even if what they are saying is true.' In this case, what one says is correct but does so offensively, and upon finding out, the subject would not like it. Back-biting is among the sins for which a person will be punished in the grave. Worse than this is *buhtān*, which is to slander. *Buhtān* means spreading a blatant lie about somebody. Another category is tattletaling: informing others about gossip that was said. This is known as *namīmah,* and is also forbidden. An example of *namīmah* is when in a gathering, somebody mentions something about someone else. People in that gathering take that gossip and spread it further by telling the victim of slander. One of the characteristics of *namīmah* is the intention to commit harm by spreading the news. The correct attitude when a gathering turns into *namīmah* is to defend the honour of the victim or at least remain quiet and hate it in the heart. The Prophet ﷺ said about the one who does this, 'The tale-bearer shall not enter Paradise.'[63] Note that this person did not start the gossip or made up lies; he only spread the gossip. Allāh takes this so seriously that He forbade this person from entering *Jannah.*

In this story, there is a clear lesson about the harms of backbiting, and of spreading rumors and gossip. This is especially the case when the crime is one of an indecent

[63] *Ṣaḥīḥ* of Muslim (196).

nature – Islam teaches us to remain quiet when a scandal occurs and try to cover up the sin rather than exacerbate it by gossiping. (Obviously, this does not apply when a crime has occurred, and the victim has the full right to expose and get the law involved.)

فَلَمَّا سَمِعَتْ بِمَكْرِهِنَّ أَرْسَلَتْ إِلَيْهِنَّ وَأَعْتَدَتْ لَهُنَّ مُتَّكَـًٔا
وَءَاتَتْ كُلَّ وَٰحِدَةٍ مِّنْهُنَّ سِكِّينًا وَقَالَتِ ٱخْرُجْ عَلَيْهِنَّ ۖ
فَلَمَّا رَأَيْنَهُۥٓ أَكْبَرْنَهُۥ وَقَطَّعْنَ أَيْدِيَهُنَّ وَقُلْنَ حَٰشَ
لِلَّهِ مَا هَٰذَا بَشَرًا إِنْ هَٰذَآ إِلَّا مَلَكٌ كَرِيمٌ ﴿٣١﴾

When she heard about their gossip, she invited them and set a banquet for them. She gave each one a knife, then said 'to Yūsuf', "Come out before them." When they saw him, they were so stunned 'by his beauty' that they cut their hands and exclaimed, "Good God! This cannot be human; this must be a noble angel!"

The wife of Al-ʿAzīz knew that the women were spreading gossip to ridicule her. She knew that they were mocking her for being powerless in the face of her passion for her slave. She decided to teach them a practical lesson about her infatuation by calling them to her home to witness the beauty of Yūsuf for themselves. ***'She invited them and set a banquet for them. She gave each one a knife...'*** The *mutaka*ʿ is translated here as a 'banquet' because of the food, but literally it means a place of rest. So, she treated them to a nice meal, and when they were reclining, she gave each of them a knife with which to cut the fruits for dessert. Then she called Yūsuf to ***'Come out before them.'*** When he presented himself, his beauty dazzled them; ***'...they were so stunned 'by his beauty' that they cut their hands...'*** In their astonishment, they cut right through the fruit, or they missed it, and cut into their own hands. It is as if they didn't even notice the pain because of their amazement and desire for him. In other words, they testified to the beauty of Yūsuf with their blood.

'Good God! This cannot be human; this must be a noble angel!' The wording here indicates the degree of their surprise. Most angels are known to be beautiful, and this statement shows us that even pagan cultures believed in this reality of the unseen. The fact that all the women lost their senses shows us that the beauty of Yūsuf was not relative, but a genuinely supernatural one. Realize that these were all married women, and typically married men and women have more control over such desires than young, unmarried people. Yet all of them, without exception, were astonished by Yūsuf's extraordinary good looks. This also shows us that illicit sexual desire is one of the most difficult tests for humans.

قَالَتْ فَذَٰلِكُنَّ ٱلَّذِى لُمْتُنَّنِى فِيهِ ۖ وَلَقَدْ رَٰوَدتُّهُۥ عَن نَّفْسِهِۦ
فَٱسْتَعْصَمَ ۖ وَلَئِن لَّمْ يَفْعَلْ مَآ ءَامُرُهُۥ لَيُسْجَنَنَّ وَلَيَكُونًا
مِّنَ ٱلصَّٰغِرِينَ ﴿٣٢﴾

She said, "This is the one for whose love you criticized me! I did try to seduce him, but he 'firmly' refused. And if he does not do what I order him to, he will certainly be imprisoned and 'fully' disgraced."

The wife of Al-ʿAzīz had achieved her aim. She had proven to her friends that in desiring Yūsuf, she was not deranged. ***'She said, "This is the one for whose love you criticized me!..."'*** It is as if she was saying, 'You see? You saw him just once and bled for him. What about the one who has to see him day and night?' Then she unashamedly admitted to her sin, and this shows us her level of depravity. ***'...I did try to seduce him but he 'firmly' refused...'*** She had lost all sense of shame and openly professed to trying to act on her lustful desire. The words she used to describe Yūsuf's response are *fa-astaʿṣam,* meaning, 'he resisted, he firmly refused, and he protected himself.' The way she described his refusal also implies that Yūsuf possessed an inner beauty, which was his modesty and morals, in addition to his external beauty. It shows us that people are attracted by inner beauty as well as outer beauty, although as Muslims, we know that inner beauty is more important.

It also shows us that Allāh knows best upon whom to confer beauty. He gave Yūsuf half of all beauty, and then tested him with temptation, but because of his strong *īmān*, Yūsuf was able to resist it. How many amongst us would have had that level of resistance? If we had possessed a fraction of Yūsuf's beauty, we would not know how to escape its temptation. We should accept what Allāh has ordained for us, believing that Allāh is the Best of all Planners. He loves us more than we love ourselves. He knows our weaknesses, and what is best for us, so let's be content with what we have. The story of Yūsuf illustrates this point for us, over and over again.

Then she gave her final ultimatum: ***'...And if he does not do what I order him to, he will certainly be imprisoned and 'fully' disgraced.'*** Now she openly threatened Yūsuf in front of the other women, saying that if he refuses her again, she will have him imprisoned. Faced with such an overwhelming situation, Yūsuf turned to Allāh.

قَالَ رَبِّ ٱلسِّجْنُ أَحَبُّ إِلَيَّ مِمَّا يَدْعُونَنِيٓ إِلَيْهِۖ وَإِلَّا تَصْرِفْ
عَنِّي كَيْدَهُنَّ أَصْبُ إِلَيْهِنَّ وَأَكُن مِّنَ ٱلْجَٰهِلِينَ ٣٣

Yūsuf prayed, "My Lord! I would rather be in jail than do what they invite me to. And if You do not turn their cunning away from me, I might yield to them and fall into ignorance."

Yūsuf knows that there is no power or strength except with Allāh, so he made a heartfelt *duʿā'*, ***'My Lord! I would rather be in jail than do what they invite me to...'*** He knew that submitting to an illicit act would lead to prison in the *Ākhirah* and that that is a far greater, more severe, and lasting punishment than the imprisonment of this world for refusing to commit immorality. On the one hand, he was invited to the most beguiling pleasure known to man, and on the other, was the threat of the worst form of physical and psychological torture. Out of fear of Allāh and hope in His reward, Yūsuf chose the latter.

'...And if You do not turn their cunning away from me, I might yield to them and fall into ignorance.' We sense the desperation in Yūsuf's choice of words. We can feel his vulnerability and his sincerity: he knows he cannot humanly avoid this temptation unless Allāh helps him in doing so. Someone who controlled his *dunyā,* meaning Al-ʿAzīz's wife, invited Yūsuf to do a sinful deed, with the implication that if he complied, she would shower him with gifts and privileges, and if not, Yūsuf should expect imprisonment and a miserable life. Allāh helped Yūsuf in this challenging situation.

Aṣbu means 'to incline towards'. Yūsuf did not want to incline towards these women because he knew that it would cause him to become one of the 'ignorant'. It is the height of ignorance that one knows the Truth, and right from wrong, and yet chooses to act contrarily. Yūsuf abhorred becoming *jāhil* or ignorant. What has 'ignorance' got to do with this crime? Some of the early scholars said anyone who disobeys Allāh is *jāhil,* in that he is acting ignorantly. The Qur'ān says that *'Allāh only accepts the repentance of those who commit evil ignorantly 'or recklessly' then repent soon after.'*[64] 'Ignorantly' here has been interpreted as someone who lapsed into sin because of weakness, but quickly turned back to Allāh in repentance and did not repeat that sin. In this sense, everyone who disobeys Allāh is a *jāhil.*

Thus, again we see that Yūsuf had perfected, by the Will of Allāh, both types of beauty.

فَٱسْتَجَابَ لَهُۥ رَبُّهُۥ فَصَرَفَ عَنْهُ كَيْدَهُنَّ ۚ إِنَّهُۥ هُوَ ٱلسَّمِيعُ ٱلْعَلِيمُ ﴿٣٤﴾

So his Lord responded to him, turning their cunning away from him. Surely He is the All-Hearing, All-Knowing.

We know that Allāh responds to those who call on Him, and He knows the sincerity of our *du'ā'*. Yūsuf called out sincerely, ***'So his Lord responded to him, turning their cunning away from him...'*** Allāh protected Yūsuf from the women's advances, and this shows us that *du'ā'* is truly the weapon of the believer. In his moment of need, Yūsuf called to Allāh for help, and He responded. The one who calls out to Allāh sincerely will always find their prayer answered, and Allāh can indeed perform miracles and

[64] *an-Nisā'* (4: 17).

provide from where one least expects. ***'...Surely He is the All-Hearing, All-Knowing.'***

ثُمَّ بَدَا لَهُم مِّنۢ بَعْدِ مَا رَأَوُا۟ ٱلْءَايَٰتِ لَيَسْجُنُنَّهُۥ حَتَّىٰ حِينٍ ﴿٣٥﴾

And so it occurred to those in charge, despite seeing all the proofs 'of his innocence', that he should be imprisoned for a while.

After this incident, and Yūsuf's sincere *du'ā'*, ***'...it occurred to those in charge, despite seeing all the proofs 'of his innocence' that he should be imprisoned for a while.'*** The 'proofs' that Allāh refers to here most likely represent Yūsuf's character. So powerful was Yūsuf's character that Allāh called it a 'sign,' which they witnessed. Although they knew that he was innocent, they decided to jail Yūsuf to calm the situation. They blamed Yūsuf, the victim, to save the reputation of the perpetrator, the wife of a powerful minister. The unjust treatment of Yūsuf reminds us that thousands of years later, there is no change in the attitude of the rich and powerful of this world: they continue to imprison the innocent to save themselves.

Yūsuf's life is a primer in patience in the face of tragedy. As a child, Yūsuf was thrown in the well, then Allāh saved him and placed him in luxury and peace. Now, Allāh was testing him again with an even more severe test: prison. It shows that tests are not a one-off experience; instead, the life of this world is a series of tests and trials. Each time a trial passes and ease comes, the next trial and ease are higher. At the end of all tests lies, for those who pass them, the greatest reward, the everlasting abode of *Jannah*.

PART FOUR

The Prisoner

وَدَخَلَ مَعَهُ ٱلسِّجْنَ فَتَيَانِ ۖ قَالَ أَحَدُهُمَآ إِنِّىٓ أَرَىٰنِىٓ أَعْصِرُ
خَمْرًا ۖ وَقَالَ ٱلْـَٔاخَرُ إِنِّىٓ أَرَىٰنِىٓ أَحْمِلُ فَوْقَ رَأْسِى خُبْزًا تَأْكُلُ
ٱلطَّيْرُ مِنْهُ ۖ نَبِّئْنَا بِتَأْوِيلِهِۦٓ ۖ إِنَّا نَرَىٰكَ مِنَ ٱلْمُحْسِنِينَ ﴿٣٦﴾

And two other servants went to jail with Yūsuf. One of them said, "I dreamt I was pressing wine." The other said, "I dreamt I was carrying 'some' bread on my head, from which birds were eating." 'Then both said,' "Tell us their interpretation, for we surely see you as one of the good-doers."

Yūsuf finds himself falsely accused and thrown into prison. Even in this bleak situation, his conduct and knowledge distinguished him from other prisoners, two of whom entered the jail at the same time as him. These were the king's breadmaker and winemaker, accused of plotting to poison the king. Because of Yūsuf's noble character, these two young prisoners drew close to him and asked him to interpret their dreams. ***'...One of them said, "I dreamt I was pressing wine." The other said, "I dreamt I was carrying 'some' bread on my head, from which birds were eating."'*** The prisoners understood that a righteous person could interpret dreams, ***'...for we surely see you as one of the good-doers.'*** They recognized that Yūsuf was from the *muḥsinīn*, the righteous. Allāh had blessed Yūsuf with wisdom, knowledge, and the ability to interpret dreams, and now it was time for him to use these gifts to help his fellow prisoners.

قَالَ لَا يَأْتِيكُمَا طَعَامٌ تُرْزَقَانِهِۦٓ إِلَّا نَبَّأْتُكُمَا بِتَأْوِيلِهِۦ قَبْلَ
أَن يَأْتِيَكُمَا ۚ ذَٰلِكُمَا مِمَّا عَلَّمَنِى رَبِّىٓ ۚ إِنِّى تَرَكْتُ مِلَّةَ قَوْمٍ
لَّا يُؤْمِنُونَ بِٱللَّهِ وَهُم بِٱلْءَاخِرَةِ هُمْ كَـٰفِرُونَ ٣٧

Yūsuf replied, "No food will come to you as your provision, but I will have informed you of its interpretation before it comes. This 'knowledge' is from what my Lord has taught me. I have shunned the faith of a people who disbelieve in Allāh and deny the Hereafter.

Yūsuf said to them, by the time their next meal arrived, he would tell them the meaning of their dreams. Yūsuf wanted to put them at ease so that they would listen to what he had to say. He had established his credentials as honest and trustworthy, and now had the right opportunity to convey his message to a captive audience. From this, we learn that whatever situation we may find ourselves in, we should try to spread Islam's message.

'...This 'knowledge' is from what my Lord has taught me..' The believer attributes all good things to Allāh, and this was the best way for Yūsuf to talk about his belief in Allāh. He told them he didn't acquire this knowledge through sorcery or on his own; it is Allāh who taught him, Who is All-Knowing.

The next sentence informs his audience why Allāh had taught Yūsuf this knowledge? ***'...I have shunned the faith of a people who disbelieve in Allāh and deny***

the Hereafter.' First, Yūsuf informed them by way of his situation, and then he demonstrated how he got to be that good: by abandoning disbelief. He used his knowledge to call them to the way of Allāh, Whom he described as the only Creator and object of worship.

This verse beautifully illustrates for us the priorities of *daʿwah*: *tawḥīd* must come first. The Prophet ﷺ further explained this priority for us in a hadith. When he was sending Muʿādh ibn Jabal to Yemen, he advised him, 'Verily, you are going to a people among the people of the Book, so call them to testify there is no God, but Allāh and that I am the Messenger of Allāh. If they accept that, then teach them that Allāh has obligated five prayers each day and night. If they accept that, then teach them that Allāh has obligated charity to be taken from the rich and given to the poor.'[65] It is a sign of wisdom that a caller to Islam teaches the people that which is most important first.

Yūsuf told them that he rejected the belief of the people of Egypt, and then explained his faith to them.

وَٱتَّبَعْتُ مِلَّةَ ءَابَآءِىٓ إِبْرَٰهِيمَ وَإِسْحَـٰقَ وَيَعْقُوبَ ۚ مَا كَانَ لَنَآ أَن
نُّشْرِكَ بِٱللَّهِ مِن شَىْءٍ ۚ ذَٰلِكَ مِن فَضْلِ ٱللَّهِ عَلَيْنَا وَعَلَى ٱلنَّاسِ
وَلَـٰكِنَّ أَكْثَرَ ٱلنَّاسِ لَا يَشْكُرُونَ ﴿٣٨﴾

I follow the faith of my fathers: Ibrāhīm, and Isḥāq, and Yaʿqūb. It is not 'right' for us to

[65] *Ṣaḥīḥ* of Muslim (19).

associate anything with Allāh 'in worship'. This is part of Allāh's grace upon us and humanity, but most people are not grateful.

Yūsuf affirmed that he was on the same religion as all the prophets of Allāh, and he had come with the same message as they. Even if they might not have heard of it before, this religion had been practiced for generations.

Then he went on to define the essence of that religion. ***'...It is not 'right' for us to associate anything with Allāh 'in worship'...'*** The phrase *min shay* here is for emphasis, meaning 'nothing whatsoever'. We associate nothing whatsoever with Allāh in our worship and, without a doubt, this was the message of all prophets. Allāh says in the Qur'ān, *'We never sent a messenger before you 'O Prophet' without revealing to him: "There is no god 'worthy of worship' except Me, so worship Me 'alone'."'*[66] In these few sentences, Yūsuf succinctly covered the three major pillars of our faith: *tawḥīd*–belief in Allāh, His Lordship, Names and Attributes and His right to be worshipped alone; *risālah*– the Message that Allāh has sent; and *Ākhirah,* the Hereafter.

'...This is part of Allāh's grace upon us and humanity, but most people are not grateful.' Yūsuf reminded his listeners that the blessings of Islam were for those who wished to take them, but most of humanity is not thankful. Despite the adversities Yūsuf experienced, he did not express any negativity about them. That he was snatched away from his father as a child, then sold into slavery, and

[66] *al-Anbiyā'* (21: 25).

then falsely accused of a crime and thrown into prison, were not necessarily bad. Instead, he dwelt on the positives that Allāh had given him: prophethood, beauty, knowledge, and worldly power. So he said, '*...This is part of Allāh's grace upon us...*' There is a profound message here, that the believers should look at the countless blessings of Allāh, which they cannot sufficiently thank Him for, instead of complaining about a few difficulties.

يَٰصَٰحِبَيِ ٱلسِّجۡنِ ءَأَرۡبَابٞ مُّتَفَرِّقُونَ خَيۡرٌ أَمِ ٱللَّهُ ٱلۡوَٰحِدُ ٱلۡقَهَّارُ ٣٩

O my fellow-prisoners! Which is far better: many different lords or Allāh – the One, the Supreme?

Yūsuf addressed his audience in beautiful terms, highlighting his shared experience with them, by saying, '***O my fellow prisoners!...***' Whenever the Qur'ān calls people to worship Allāh, it uses terms like 'O mankind!' or 'O children of Ādam' or 'O People of the Book.' It uses disparaging terms only when the disbelievers ask the Prophet to compromise *tawḥīd*. Then the response is, 'O you who disbelieve, I worship not what you worship;'[67] or 'Is it other than Allāh you order me to worship, O you ignorant ones?'[68] Here, Yūsuf was alluding to the circumstantial bond between them, so it created affinity, and his invitation became appealing.

[67] *al-Kāfirūn* (109: 1-2).
[68] *al-Zumar* (39: 64).

'...Which is far better: many different lords or Allāh – the One, the Supreme?' After preaching to them about the Oneness of Allāh, Yūsuf now challenged them directly, yet most nobly and sensibly, because sometimes directness is needed. Too often, we avoid frank and straightforward talk because we don't want to appear politically incorrect. The people of Egypt were idolaters, and Yūsuf appealed to their *fiṭrah* or original nature. 'Are many different gods better? Or One Who rules Supreme?' In so doing, he referred to the Oneness of Allāh's Lordship (*Tawḥīd al-Rubūbiyyah*), and the Oneness of Allāh's Name and Attributes (*Tawḥīd al-Asmā' wa-Siffāt*). He also mentioned two beautiful names of Allāh: *Al-Wāḥid,* 'the One,' meaning 'there is nothing like Him'; and *Al-Qahhār,* 'the Supreme,' meaning 'the One who conquers all else,' and is more powerful than any king. He also used a rhetorical question, which was perfect for this occasion.

مَا تَعْبُدُونَ مِن دُونِهِۦٓ إِلَّآ أَسْمَآءً سَمَّيْتُمُوهَآ أَنتُمْ وَءَابَآؤُكُم
مَّآ أَنزَلَ ٱللَّهُ بِهَا مِن سُلْطَٰنٍ ۚ إِنِ ٱلْحُكْمُ إِلَّا لِلَّهِ ۚ أَمَرَ أَلَّا تَعْبُدُوٓا۟
إِلَّآ إِيَّاهُ ۚ ذَٰلِكَ ٱلدِّينُ ٱلْقَيِّمُ وَلَٰكِنَّ أَكْثَرَ ٱلنَّاسِ لَا يَعْلَمُونَ ﴿٤٠﴾

Whatever 'idols' you worship instead of Him are mere names which you and your forefathers have made up – a practice Allāh has never authorized. It is only Allāh Who decides. He has commanded that you worship none but Him. That is the upright faith, but most people do not know.

Speaking frankly, Yūsuf now told his fellow inmates that they worshipped gods whom they had created and given their names. That what they did was ***'...a practice Allāh has never authorized. It is only Allāh Who decides...'*** In a balancing act, Yūsuf politely but candidly told them that all religions were not the same. He did not mince his words when defending the Oneness and Almightiness of Allāh. We can use this verse to reply to those who say it doesn't matter which way you worship Allāh, that all religions are valid. In truth, only that for which Allāh has sent down authority, has sanctioned and legislated, is the right religion. The *ḥukm* or judgement and ruling in this matter is only for Allāh. Only He has the right to legislate what is permissible or impermissible.

'...He has commanded that you worship none but Him. That is the upright faith, but most people do not know.' Yūsuf now called to the Oneness of Allāh in Worship (*Tawḥīd al-Ulūhiyyah)*, the third aspect of *tawḥīd*, saying Allāh has commanded you to worship Him Alone, and that Islam is the only right religion, even though most people do not know. It was the height of eloquence. Yūsuf had given a comprehensive *daʿwah* in a few words. We can learn about content, methodology, psychology, and strategy of *daʿwah* from Yūsuf's approach.

Also, the callers to Islam must establish their credentials through good conduct and manners. Their actions should speak louder than words. They should be approachable, easy-going, and gentle. When giving *daʿwah*, they should address people with respect, highlighting commonalities, and using emotional and logical arguments to drive the point. Callers to Islam need to know their audience, their history, and their theologies so they can explain to their peoples how their faith evolved.

Another interesting point here is that we should criticize the action, not the person. Yūsuf said he would never commit idolatry, but did not lambast his fellow prisoners for doing so. Even under challenging circumstances, Yūsuf made it a priority to benefit others and make sure he spread the message of Islam.

يَٰصَٰحِبَيِ ٱلسِّجۡنِ أَمَّآ أَحَدُكُمَا فَيَسۡقِي رَبَّهُۥ خَمۡرٗاۖ وَأَمَّا ٱلۡأٓخَرُ فَيُصۡلَبُ فَتَأۡكُلُ ٱلطَّيۡرُ مِن رَّأۡسِهِۦۚ قُضِيَ ٱلۡأَمۡرُ ٱلَّذِي فِيهِ تَسۡتَفۡتِيَانِ ٤١

O my fellow-prisoners! 'The first' one of you will serve wine to his master, and the other will be crucified, and the birds will eat from his head. The matter about which you inquired has been decided.

The Qur'ān does not tell us if the prisoners accepted Islam, and this shows that conversion shouldn't be our main concern. The primary goal should be to present Islam in the best manner possible, without compromise. When the goal is merely to convert the person, we become at risk of bending Islam's teachings to fit with that person's concept of right and wrong. We should understand that a person's understanding may not be perfect, but Allāh's *Dīn* is. Our goal is to present the Truth in the best manner, whether or not people accept it.

Yūsuf then moved on to their dreams. Addressing them with terms of endearment, he said, ***'O my fellow-prisoners! 'The first' one of you…'*** Out of politeness, he did not say which prisoner, because he was about to deliver bad news. ***'…will serve wine to his master, and the other will be crucified, and the birds will eat from his head…'*** How did Yūsuf come to this conclusion? The first dream was relatively straightforward, indicating that the winemaker will be released and return to his role serving the King. In the second, the scholars say that the bread that the birds were eating represented the face of the breadmaker, his body left lying unburied, as happened after a crucifixion. Yūsuf ended this interpretation with a factual statement: ***'…The matter about which you inquired has been decided.'*** Notice here that only a prophet of Allāh could interpret a dream with such certainty.

وَقَالَ لِلَّذِى ظَنَّ أَنَّهُۥ نَاجٍ مِّنْهُمَا ٱذْكُرْنِى عِندَ رَبِّكَ فَأَنسَىٰهُ
ٱلشَّيْطَٰنُ ذِكْرَ رَبِّهِۦ فَلَبِثَ فِى ٱلسِّجْنِ بِضْعَ سِنِينَ ﴿٤٢﴾

Then he said to the one he knew would survive, "Mention me in the presence of your master." But Shayṭān made him forget to mention Yūsuf to his master, so he remained in prison for several years.

Yūsuf then turned to the one who will be released, the winemaker, and said, *'...Mention me in the presence of your master...'* He asked the prisoner to remind the King that he was still in prison. We see from this that it is allowed to ask for help. *Tawakkul*, trust in Allāh, involves relying on Allāh while also taking the necessary means. Yūsuf didn't just sit back and rely on his *du'ā'*; he also used the means available to him. Asking others for help while putting our trust in Allāh was the way of our Prophet ﷺ. The entire *Sīrah* from beginning to end indicates that he didn't just rely on prayer; he ﷺ also built coalitions and alliances, sought personal protection, waged defensive wars, and signed treaties to achieve his goal. From this, we learn that it is a *Sunnah* to use all permissible means in the furtherance of our legitimate objectives. Just as Yūsuf wanted his case to go before the King to regain freedom, we have every right to take our issues to the courts and use whatever means at our disposal to protect our rights.

'...But Shayṭān made him forget to mention Yūsuf to his master...' One of *Shayṭān*'s tricks is to make us forget something important, and it is from the Mercy of Allāh that He does not take us to account for things we forget. *Shayṭān* made the winemaker engrossed in his new-found freedom, and he forgot to mention Yūsuf to the King. ***'... so he remained in prison for several years...'*** Allāh says *biḍ'i sinīn,* which is between three and nine years. Most of the scholars say Yūsuf spent seven more years in prison for a crime he did not commit. Some may think of it as gross injustice to Yūsuf, but it was all part of Allāh's Divine wisdom. A relative hardship can entail an immense benefit. Yūsuf would not have attained the high position had he been released earlier. Allāh told us, *'With hardship comes ease,'* and a hadith expounded on it thus: "Know that there is much good in being patient with what you detest, victory will come with patience, affliction will come with relief, and 'with hardship will come ease.'"[69]

Here, it should be mentioned that another interpretation also exists of this verse, but this interpretation only stems from an incorrect understanding of *tawakkul*, or trust in Allāh. Some early authors felt that Yūsuf had somehow committed an offense by asking another person to help him, instead of asking Allāh. Hence, they would translate the pronouns in this verse differently, as follows, "Then he said to the one he knew would survive, 'Mention me in the presence of your master.' But *Shayṭān* made Yūsuf forget to remember Allāh, so he remained in prison for several years." In this other interpretation, it is as if Yūsuf is being 'punished' by Allāh for daring to ask a fellow-prisoner to intercede. However, this interpretation is simply false. We are expected to use every permissible means at our disposal to arrive at our intended result, and Allāh's blessings will only come if we strive and act, not if we just sit back and do nothing. Even the miracles of the prophet's required some action to spark or begin the miracle!

---

[69] *Musnad* of Aḥmad (2800).

PART FIVE

The King and His Dream

وَقَالَ ٱلْمَلِكُ إِنِّىٓ أَرَىٰ سَبْعَ بَقَرَٰتٍ سِمَانٍ يَأْكُلُهُنَّ سَبْعٌ عِجَافٌ
وَسَبْعَ سُنۢبُلَٰتٍ خُضْرٍ وَأُخَرَ يَابِسَٰتٍ ۖ يَٰٓأَيُّهَا ٱلْمَلَأُ أَفْتُونِى فِى
رُءْيَٰىَ إِن كُنتُمْ لِلرُّءْيَا تَعْبُرُونَ ﴿٤٣﴾

And 'one day' the King said, "I dreamt of seven fat cows eaten up by seven skinny ones; and seven green ears of grain and 'seven' others dry. O chiefs! Tell me the meaning of my dream if you can interpret dreams."

While Yūsuf was still in prison, the King of Egypt saw a dream which shook him. ***'The King said, "I dreamt of seven fat cows eaten up by seven skinny ones, and seven green ears of grain and 'seven' others dry."'*** Allāh referred to him as *Al-Malik,* which means 'the King', and not *Fir'awn* or Pharaoh. There is no mention of Pharaoh in the story of Yūsuf, yet when Allāh talked about the Prophet Mūsā, He used the term Pharaoh for the ruler. The Bible refers to both rulers as Pharaoh. So why does the Qur'ān differentiate?

The reason is that Egypt had two kingdoms–the Upper and Lower. Some scholars said the city in which Yūsuf had settled was the capital of the Upper Middle Kingdom, the ancient city of Manf or Memphis. Historians say that the rulers at the time of Yūsuf did not use the title Pharaoh because they were from the Hyksos dynasty, outsiders who had invaded Egypt. The rulers of Egypt at the time of Mūsā were from an indigenous Egyptian dynasty, and they referred to themselves as Pharaohs. The Pharaonic dynasty had ended long before the Prophet's ﷺ arrival, and there is no way he could have known the distinction between the two ruling families. The Qur'ān's careful differentiation between the two rulers proves that it is from Allāh; the Bible does not point out this critical distinction.

The King gathered his ministers, ***'O chiefs! Tell me the meaning of my dream if you can interpret dreams.'***

قَالُوٓا۟ أَضْغَٰثُ أَحْلَٰمٍ ۖ وَمَا نَحْنُ بِتَأْوِيلِ ٱلْأَحْلَٰمِ بِعَٰلِمِينَ ﴿٤٤﴾

They replied, "These are confused visions and we do not know the interpretation of such dreams."

The King called his dream a *ru'yā* or a positive dream, but the elders said, ***'These are confused visions…,'*** calling it *aḥlām*. The use of two different terms indicates that the King felt his dream had significance, while his ministers thought it was false and confusing and hence had no deeper meaning to it.

'…and we do not know the interpretation of such dreams.' The ministers tried to save face by saying that had it been a true *ru'yā,* they would have been able to interpret it. Most ignorant people never admit their ignorance, but instead, seek to justify it with concocted statements.

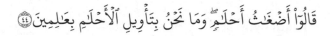

وَقَالَ ٱلَّذِى نَجَا مِنْهُمَا وَٱدَّكَرَ بَعْدَ أُمَّةٍ أَنَا۠ أُنَبِّئُكُم
بِتَأْوِيلِهِۦ فَأَرْسِلُونِ ﴿٤٥﴾

'Finally,' the surviving ex-prisoner remembered 'Yūsuf' after a long time and said, "I will tell you its interpretation, so send me forth 'to Yūsuf'."

The news spread that the King had seen a dream which none of his ministers had been able to interpret. At this point, the winemaker eventually remembered Yūsuf, who had interpreted his and the other man's dream accurately. The use of the term ***'...after a time...'*** implies that he should have remembered long ago, so he said, ***"I will tell you its interpretation, so send me forth 'to Yūsuf'."*** He must have used this opportunity to make his presence known to the King, and to tell the King of his strange and interesting friend who had interpreted his own dream so many years ago. Therefore, he asked for permission to go to the prison to ask Yūsuf for his interpretation of the King's dream.

يُوسُفُ أَيُّهَا ٱلصِّدِّيقُ أَفْتِنَا فِى سَبْعِ بَقَرَٰتٍ سِمَانٍ يَأْكُلُهُنَّ
سَبْعٌ عِجَافٌ وَسَبْعِ سُنۢبُلَٰتٍ خُضْرٍ وَأُخَرَ يَابِسَٰتٍ لَّعَلِّىٓ أَرْجِعُ
إِلَى ٱلنَّاسِ لَعَلَّهُمْ يَعْلَمُونَ ﴿٤٦﴾

He said, "Yūsuf, O man of truth! Interpret for us 'the dream of' seven fat cows having been eaten up by seven skinny ones; and seven green ears of grain and 'seven' others dry, so that I may return to the people and let them know."

Seven years had passed since Yūsuf asked the winemaker to mention him to the King, but when the winemaker came to Yūsuf to ask for a favour, he offered no apology for forgetting the request. Still, Yūsuf, a man of exemplary character, did not turn him away or reprimand him. The winemaker called Yūsuf a *ṣiddīq*, ***'... man of truth...,'*** because he had witnessed Yūsuf's honesty and truthfulness in the shared jail cell and how accurately the latter had interpreted his dream.

Recounting the King's dream, the winemaker implored Yūsuf, ***'...Interpret for us 'the dream of' seven fat cows eaten up by seven skinny ones, and seven green ears of grain and 'seven' others dry.'*** As we will see, the seven fat cows symbolized seven years of abundant crops, and the seven lean ones seven years of drought. He said, ***'...so that I may return to the people and let them know.'*** What he implied was that doing so would also inform them about Yūsuf's excellence in dream interpretation and remind them of his plight.

Notice as well that the winemaker conveniently forgets to tell Yūsuf that this dream is from the King himself! Obviously, the winemaker wants to take full credit and perhaps get monetary reward, and he feels that telling Yūsuf such details might make Yūsuf want some of what the winemaker wanted. But Yūsuf is not interested in such petty games!

قَالَ تَزْرَعُونَ سَبْعَ سِنِينَ دَأَبًا فَمَا حَصَدتُّمْ فَذَرُوهُ فِي سُنۢبُلِهِۦٓ إِلَّا قَلِيلًا مِّمَّا تَأْكُلُونَ ﴿٤٧﴾

Yūsuf replied, "You will plant 'grain' for seven consecutive years, leaving in the ear whatever you will harvest, except for the little you will eat.

Yūsuf not only interpreted the dream but also suggested the remedy. ***'…You will plant 'grain' for seven consecutive years, leaving in the ear whatever you will harvest, except for the little you will eat.'*** Yūsuf advised them that the first seven years, they should only eat what was necessary to sustain their lives and leave the rest in the stalks. Even though Yūsuf was in jail, Allāh put him in a commanding position where he was telling the king through the winemaker what to do. By offering them a solution, he went above and beyond what the winemaker had requested him to do. It was the height of good manners and showed his sincerity to Allāh. The Prophet ﷺ said, 'I am amazed at the patience of my brother Yūsuf, and his generosity and Allāh will forgive him. When he was asked to interpret the dream, I would not have done so until they let me out.'[70]

[70] *Muʿjam al-Kabīr* of al-Ṭabaranī (1945).

In other words, the Prophet ﷺ said he would have demanded freedom in return for interpreting the dream, but Yūsuf did not put forth such a condition.

ثُمَّ يَأْتِي مِنۢ بَعْدِ ذَٰلِكَ سَبْعٌ شِدَادٌ يَأْكُلْنَ مَا قَدَّمْتُمْ لَهُنَّ
إِلَّا قَلِيلًا مِّمَّا تُحْصِنُونَ ﴿٤٨﴾

Then after that will come seven years of great hardship which will consume whatever you have saved, except the little you will store 'for seed'.

Yūsuf told them that after seven years of the bumper harvest will come seven tough years when the crops will fail, and food would run short. ***"...which will consume whatever you have saved, except the little you will store 'for seed'."*** Then the people would need to survive on what was saved in previous years, other than the seed for the next planting.

ثُمَّ يَأْتِي مِنۢ بَعْدِ ذَٰلِكَ عَامٌ فِيهِ يُغَاثُ ٱلنَّاسُ وَفِيهِ يَعْصِرُونَ ﴿٤٩﴾

Then after that will come a year in which people will receive abundant rain and they will press 'oil and wine'."

Yūsuf said that after these fourteen years will come a year in which rainfall shall be abundant, ***"...and they will press 'oil and wine'."*** Meaning, the rain will be so plentiful that they will be able to grow abundant fruits, including grapes, from which to extract oil and wine. Since wine is a luxury, its extraction indicates plentifulness. People don't press wine if there is not enough to eat.

The dream does not mention a year of abundant produce and pressing of wines, but Yūsuf talks about them matter of factly. The question is, how did Yūsuf deduce it from the dream? The extra details Yūsuf filled in showed the depth of his understanding. He figured that after seven years of drought, there must be a surplus of rain, or else the drought would not end.

In Yūsuf's detailed advice for the King, we see his concern for humanity. He didn't withhold beneficial information from a people who were not just idol worshipers, but also his oppressors. He valued their life as fellow humans, and this is what Islam advocates; Allāh wants the believers to be merciful so they may receive His mercy.

When the King's envoy returned to the King and informed him about Yūsuf's interpretation, the King became filled with curiosity. Who is this man? What is his story?

And so, Allāh worked in His own ways to bring the matter of the boy in the well directly into the court of the King of Egypt. When Allāh is on your side, miracles occur, and protection is given, and change happens from sources no one could have predicted.

PART SIX

From Prisoner to Minister

وَقَالَ ٱلْمَلِكُ ٱئْتُونِى بِهِۦ ۖ فَلَمَّا جَآءَهُ ٱلرَّسُولُ قَالَ ٱرْجِعْ إِلَىٰ
رَبِّكَ فَسْـَٔلْهُ مَا بَالُ ٱلنِّسْوَةِ ٱلَّـٰتِى قَطَّعْنَ أَيْدِيَهُنَّ ۚ إِنَّ
رَبِّى بِكَيْدِهِنَّ عَلِيمٌ ﴿٥٠﴾

The King 'then' said, "Bring him to me." When the messenger came to him, Yūsuf said, "Go back to your master and ask him about the case of the women who cut their hands. Surely my Lord has 'full' knowledge of their cunning."

The King ordered that Yūsuf be released and brought back to him in the palace. Any person in Yūsuf's situation would have jumped at the news (after all, he had suffered prolonged imprisonment), but not he. Instead, Yūsuf said, ***'...Go back to your master and ask him about the case of the women who cut their hands...'*** Even the Prophet ﷺ expressed admiration for the patience of Yūsuf!

Yūsuf was serving time for an alleged moral crime, which the Egyptian society of the time did not consider that serious. They had not accused him of a crime like murder or theft. Yet, Yūsuf wanted the accusation to be expunged from his record because he cared about his honour. Being accused of immorality was a greater punishment for him than imprisonment.

Here again, Yūsuf showed a high standard. He asked about the women who cut their hands and not the wife of Al-'Azīz. There are two reasons for this. First, he did not want to go into explicit details of the case and thereby directly point fingers at Al-ʿAzīz's wife. Second, Yūsuf, by using cryptic language, wanted to arouse the curiosity of the King so the latter could investigate and find out the truth himself. Sure enough, the plan worked.

قَالَ مَا خَطْبُكُنَّ إِذْ رَٰوَدتُّنَّ يُوسُفَ عَن نَّفْسِهِۦ ۚ قُلْنَ حَٰشَ لِلَّهِ مَا عَلِمْنَا عَلَيْهِ مِن سُوٓءٍ ۚ قَالَتِ ٱمْرَأَتُ ٱلْعَزِيزِ ٱلْـَٰٔنَ حَصْحَصَ ٱلْحَقُّ أَنَا۠ رَٰوَدتُّهُۥ عَن نَّفْسِهِۦ وَإِنَّهُۥ لَمِنَ ٱلصَّٰدِقِينَ ﴿٥١﴾

The King asked 'the women', "What did you get when you tried to seduce Yūsuf?" They replied, "Allāh forbid! We know nothing indecent about him." Then the Chief Minister's wife admitted, "Now the truth has come to light. It was I who tried to seduce him, and he is surely truthful.

The King invited all the women to the palace, as well as the wife of Al-ʿAzīz. The plan of the Divine works in wondrous ways. Had the King not needed his dream's interpretation, he would never have become involved with such a petty issue. It is of Allāh's wisdom that this matter landed in the highest court in Egypt. The King now had a personal interest in the case, which would lead him to discover Yūsuf's innocence, his nobility, and talents.

This King asked the women, ***'What did you get when you tried to seduce Yūsuf?'*** although the charge was not against the women who had cut their hands but against Yūsuf and the wife of Al-ʿAzīz. These women were not guilty of any crime other than trying to coax Yūsuf, but the King wanted to know what happened and why. ***'...They replied, "Allāh forbid!..."'*** They tried to clear themselves, first by using the phrase: *ḥāshalillāh!* Which is like saying *subḥānAllāh!* or *astaghfirullāh!* By expressing amazement at the question, they said they could have never even imagined trying to seduce Yūsuf. 'God forbid! How could you accuse us of that?' Then they defended Yūsuf, ***'We know nothing indecent about him...'***

When all of them had testified that Yūsuf was of good character, there was only one person left: the wife of Al-ʿAzīz. Now, it was her turn to speak. She said, ***'Now, the truth has come to light...'*** *Haṣhaṣa* means 'it is now clear'. Everybody had testified, and she couldn't go against their testimonies; the only option left for her was to confess. Almost a decade had passed since the incident, and some scholars say that Al-ʿAzīz had even passed away. Finally, she admitted for the record: ***'It was I who tried to seduce him, and he is surely truthful.'***

ذَٰلِكَ لِيَعْلَمَ أَنِّي لَمْ أَخُنْهُ بِٱلْغَيْبِ وَأَنَّ ٱللَّهَ لَا يَهْدِي
كَيْدَ ٱلْخَآئِنِينَ ﴿٥٢﴾

From this, he should know that I did not betray him in his absence, for Allāh certainly does not guide the scheming of the dishonest.

There are different opinions as to who said this, and about whom, but the most reliable interpretation is that the speaker is Al-ʿAzīz's wife and the subject is her husband. (Some have claimed that the speaker was Yūsuf himself, and he is referring to the fact that he didn't 'betray' his master's trust, or that he didn't disobey Allāh – but the context doesn't seem to support these interpretations). She wanted to clarify, ***'I did not betray him in his absence…'*** And that is because, even though she planned to do so, she did not physically commit the deed. Perhaps until his dying day, Al-ʿAzīz had doubts about the loyalty of his wife. Now she said, 'I am saying this so that the truth be known. I was loyal to him. I did not betray his trust.' Even though she had pleaded not guilty to the sin, she had confessed to trying to do so.

وَمَآ أُبَرِّئُ نَفْسِيٓۚ إِنَّ ٱلنَّفْسَ لَأَمَّارَةُۢ بِٱلسُّوٓءِ إِلَّا مَا رَحِمَ رَبِّيٓۚ
إِنَّ رَبِّي غَفُورٞ رَّحِيمٞ ٥٣

And I do not seek to free myself from blame, for indeed the soul is ever inclined to evil, except for those shown mercy by my Lord. Surely my Lord is All-Forgiving, Most Merciful."

All this time, the wife of Al-ʿAzīz must have lived with an enormous sense of guilt; not only had she brought disrepute to herself and her husband, but she had also sent an innocent person to prison for many years. Now was the time to clear her conscience, so she said, ***'And I do not seek to free myself from blame…'*** She blamed this lapse on her soul. ***'…for indeed, the soul is ever inclined to evil, except those shown mercy by my Lord…'*** It's like she was saying, 'It wasn't my fault. It was beyond my control; I couldn't help it! Sometimes our passions and souls overtake us and command us to do evil.' ***'…Surely my Lord is All-Forgiving, Most Merciful.'*** In other words: 'I hope that my Lord will forgive me.'

The notion of the soul commanding the body to do evil is a point that deserves reflection. Does our soul order us to do evil? Scholars have defined three categories of the human soul:

1. **The Inciting Soul (*An-Nafs al-'Ammārah*):** This soul does not have faith in Allāh, and it is the type of soul the wife of Al-ʿAzīz referred to here. Because of the absence of faith–the moral compass–there is nothing to keep the sinful attitude of this type of soul. The bearer of this soul may commit evil actions recklessly without feeling remorse.

2. **The Soul that is at Peace (*An-Nafs al-Muṭma'innah*):** This is the soul of the contented believer. It dwells in peace and certainty with its Lord and therefore does not incline towards evil. Allāh refers to this type of soul in Sūrah al-Fajr, *'Allāh will say to the righteous, "O tranquil soul! Return to your Lord, well pleased*

'with Him' and well-pleasing 'to Him''[71] Because it has reached such a lofty state, this type of soul is worthy of the highest reward.

3. **The Self-Reproaching Soul (*An-Nafs al-Lawwāmah*):** This type of soul is between ***An-Nafs al-'Ammārah*** and ***An-Nafs al-Muṭama'innah,*** and we find its reference in Sūrah al-Qiyāmah: *'And I swear by the reproaching soul.'* It has belief, but not firmly content and given to making mistakes; it teeters between faith and desires. It faces an internal struggle and reproaches itself for having done wrong. Most Muslims have this type of soul.

There is also another opinion that these three types of souls, in reality, represent phases of a single soul, which is why at times, we are at peace, at times in self-reproach, and at other times we desire evil. Both interpretations (*viz.,* that these are three different types of souls or three states of the same soul) are valid.

We believe that Allāh created all humans with pure souls because the Prophet ﷺ told us, 'No child is born but that he is upon the *fiṭrah.*'[72] The *fiṭrah,* or original nature of the human being, instinctively knows right from wrong. No human has been created evil by nature. When a person has faith in Allāh, the soul inclines towards good; but when faith leaves the heart, the soul inclines towards evil.

---

[71] *al-Fajr* (89: 27-28).

[72] *Ṣaḥīḥ* of al-Bukhārī (1292).

وَقَالَ ٱلْمَلِكُ ٱئْتُونِى بِهِۦٓ أَسْتَخْلِصْهُ لِنَفْسِى ۖ فَلَمَّا كَلَّمَهُۥ قَالَ إِنَّكَ ٱلْيَوْمَ لَدَيْنَا مَكِينٌ أَمِينٌ ﴿٥٤﴾

The King said, "Bring him to me. I will employ him exclusively in my service." And when Yūsuf spoke to him, the King said, "Today you are highly esteemed and fully trusted by us."

The King now said, ***'Bring him to me. I will employ him exclusively in my service.'*** Earlier, the King had said simply, 'Bring him to me,' but now, after investigating Yūsuf's case, he was convinced of the latter's innocence and nobility, without even meeting him. He immediately decided to induct Yūsuf into his close circle of advisers. Yūsuf's patience and sincerity had finally paid off.

Upon Yūsuf's arrival in the palace, the King exonerated him, saying, ***'Today, you are highly esteemed and fully trusted by us.'*** Yūsuf was now officially a *makīn*, honourable, and *amīn*, trustworthy. The King was so impressed that he offered him a position in his cabinet. It is a beautiful finale to the cycle of trial and temptation, redemption, and elevation. Yūsuf started in the loving care of his father, then became afflicted with several trials: thrown in a well, sold into slavery, falsely accused of seduction, wrongfully imprisoned, and lifted from the hardship and squalor of the prison to the inner circle of the King. This extraordinary story indeed shows us the nature of the life of this world.

Every new trial is bigger than the one that preceded it, but the resulting victory is twice as sweet.

قَالَ ٱجْعَلْنِي عَلَىٰ خَزَآئِنِ ٱلْأَرْضِ إِنِّي حَفِيظٌ عَلِيمٌ ﴿٥٥﴾

Yūsuf proposed, "Put me in charge of the store-houses of the land, for I am a knowing guardian."

With the insight Yūsuf had gained from interpreting the King's dream, he knew the challenges that lay ahead. He asked to be put in charge of the grain storehouses of Egypt, saying, ***'...I am a knowing guardian'*** meaning that he was a man who knew how to handle these matters, *ʿalīm*, and he could guard and protect well what was in his charge, *ḥafīdh*. These two qualities of Yūsuf shone a light on his character and worldly skills, the right balance between inner and outer spheres. A human being needs both to succeed.

What is worth noting is that Yūsuf had asked to become a minister in a non-Muslim government, so that he may use his skills to help the people. From this, we can derive that Islam encourages striving for the betterment of our societies in whatever way possible. There is no harm in working for a non-Islamic government as long as it benefits the community at large and does not hinder our religious practices or harm our beliefs. Merely working within a system that might have some evil in it does not automatically imply our endorsement of that system.

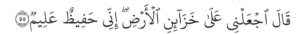

There needs to be a reasonable balance in this regard, and scholars of every land and era should set out the parameters of involvement with the systems of that time.

وَكَذَٰلِكَ مَكَّنَّا لِيُوسُفَ فِي ٱلْأَرْضِ يَتَبَوَّأُ مِنْهَا حَيْثُ يَشَآءُۚ
نُصِيبُ بِرَحْمَتِنَا مَن نَّشَآءُۖ وَلَا نُضِيعُ أَجْرَ ٱلْمُحْسِنِينَ ٥٦

This is how We established Yūsuf in the land to settle wherever he pleased. We shower Our mercy on whomever We will, and We never discount the reward of the righteous.

Again, we return to this beautiful phrase, ***'This is how We established Yūsuf in the land...'*** We first encountered it when Yūsuf was a child, and Allāh relieved him of his trial by taking him to the house of Al-ʿAzīz, *'This is how We established Yūsuf in the land so that We might teach him the interpretation of dreams.'*[73]

Yūsuf was now the most powerful minister in all of Egypt. He could travel anywhere he liked with his entourage and, ***'...settle wherever he pleased...'*** He had gone from being a prisoner to being the most powerful man in the land after the King. In some ways, he was even more powerful than the King because he controlled the nation's food supply; everyone needs food, but everyone does not necessarily require a king. The scholars say that

[73] *Yūsuf* (12: 21).

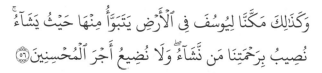

Yūsuf implemented an efficient management programme. He gathered all the grain and stored what remained after the basic needs. For seven years, people handed their produce to the government so it could be saved and stored for the seven years of impending drought.

The main reason Yūsuf deserved this massive reward was his righteousness. Allāh said, ***'...We shower Our mercy on whomever We will, and We never discount the reward of the righteous...'*** This is a fundamental lesson for us. When we are righteous, Allāh will reward us. He would never allow the good deeds of the righteous to go to waste.

وَلَأَجْرُ ٱلْـَٔاخِرَةِ خَيْرٌ لِّلَّذِينَ ءَامَنُوا۟ وَكَانُوا۟ يَتَّقُونَ ٥٧

And the reward of the Hereafter is far better for those who are faithful and are mindful 'of Allāh'.

With his power, wealth, and privilege, Yūsuf was now truly 'established in the land.' But Allāh reminds us not to be fooled by the illusions of wealth and status of this word, because they are short-lived, and because ***'...the reward of the Hereafter is far better...'*** It surpasses any of the rewards of this world, and it is more lasting. Allāh reserved these prizes exclusively for an elite minority, ***'...those who are faithful and are mindful 'of Allāh'.'***

Sufyān ibn ʿUyaynah (d. 814), and other scholars of the past used this verse as evidence that the believers will get two rewards for their good deeds: once in this world, and a second time in the Hereafter. On the other hand, Allāh will reward the disbelievers for their beneficial work only in this world, but give them nothing of the eternal blessings of the Hereafter because the prize of the everlasting life is reserved only for the believers. The disbelievers will come to know the severity of their loss on the Day of Judgement, but such a realization will be too late.

PART SEVEN

The Brothers Return

وَجَآءَ إِخۡوَةُ يُوسُفَ فَدَخَلُواْ عَلَيۡهِ فَعَرَفَهُمۡ وَهُمۡ لَهُۥ مُنكِرُونَ ٥٨

And Yūsuf's brothers came and entered his presence. He recognized them but they were unaware of who he really was.

Allāh says, ***'And Yūsuf's brothers came…'*** From these four words, we can derive the missing scenes and appreciate the miracle of the Qur'ānic language. It was now probably the sixth year of famine. The drought had spread throughout Egypt and into the surrounding lands, including Palestine. The resulting shortage of food was so acute that people had ventured far away from home to Egypt to get grain. Due to Yūsuf's ingenious planning, there was no starvation in Egypt; in fact, they had a bit of a surplus. The King must have now practically understood what Yūsuf meant when he said at the time of asking for the finance minister's position–*'I am a knowing guardian.'*[74]

'…and entered his presence…' Not everybody would be trading directly with Yūsuf as he was the minister, but because the brothers were foreigners, they required a higher authorization, and they wanted a massive quantity of grain because of the large size of their clan. ***'…He recognized them, but they were unaware of who he really was.'*** They were his older brothers; how could Yūsuf not recognize them? Their dress was similar to his peoples', and they spoke his native Hebrew. But they had no idea

---

74 *Yūsuf* (12: 55).

that this was Yūsuf. The last time they saw him, he was a young boy of seven, and now he was a fully-grown man. How could they have imagined that their little brother not only survived but had become the second most powerful man in Egypt?

The scholars say that when Yūsuf recognized them, he began to question them, 'Who are you? Why have you come to our land?' And so they told him, 'We are a group of people living in Palestine. We are all brothers, and we have an elderly father.' Yūsuf kept questioning them until he got full news of the long-separated family.

وَلَمَّا جَهَّزَهُم بِجَهَازِهِمْ قَالَ ٱئْتُونِى بِأَخٍ لَّكُم مِّنْ أَبِيكُمْ ۚ
أَلَا تَرَوْنَ أَنِّىٓ أُوفِى ٱلْكَيْلَ وَأَنَا۠ خَيْرُ ٱلْمُنزِلِينَ ٥٩

When he had provided them with their supplies, he demanded, "Bring me your brother on your father's side. Do you not see that I give full measure, and I am the best of hosts?

The brothers are said to have stayed in Egypt for a few days, and Yūsuf treated them honourably and generously. He then helped them to prepare for their return to Palestine and ***'...provided them with their supplies...'*** meaning he even gave them additional provisions they needed for the journey. So after Yūsuf had given them all of their grain, he gave them some extra.

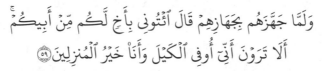

Then he said, ***'Bring me your brother on your father's side...,'*** as if Yūsuf was telling them, 'I don't know if you are telling the truth about the size of your family. You are saying you have an eleventh brother, so bring him to me next time.' He then enticed them ***'...Do you not see that I give full measure, and I am the best of hosts?'*** Nobody could surpass the quantity of grain Yūsuf had given them, and the hospitality he had showered upon them. Even though they came as merchants, he hosted them and gave them food and drink and a place to stay. Then, he gave them a final ultimatum to ensure that they came back with his full brother, Binyāmīn.

فَإِن لَّمْ تَأْتُونِي بِهِۦ فَلَا كَيْلَ لَكُمْ عِندِى وَلَا تَقْرَبُونِ ۝٦٠

But if you do not bring him to me 'next time', I will have no grain for you, nor will you ever come close to me again."

Yūsuf let them know, in no uncertain terms, that they would be unable to get grain unless they brought their youngest brother. First, an incentive, then a warning: ***'...if you do not bring him to me 'next time', I will have no grain for you...'*** It seems evident that Yūsuf was determined to get Binyāmīn to the palace. But won't that deprive his father of the second most-beloved son? The scholars have discussed many reasons as to why Yūsuf would do this, but the most logical seems to be that Allāh inspired him and that it was part of the Divine Plan. What was the wisdom?

Allāh knows best, but perhaps it was to affirm Ya'qūb's faith in Allāh, or because Yūsuf feared the brothers were not treating Binyāmīn well.

قَالُواْ سَنُرَٰوِدُ عَنۡهُ أَبَاهُ وَإِنَّا لَفَٰعِلُونَ ٦١

They promised, "We will try to convince his father to let him come. We will certainly do 'our best'."

They said, ***'We will try to convince his father to let him come...'*** Notice they said, '*his* father' and not '*our* father'. We can sense the jealousy. They knew how much Ya'qūb loved Binyāmīn and that he might not let him go with them. After what had happened to Yūsuf, how could Ya'qūb trust them with Binyāmīn?

Nonetheless, they promised, ***"...We will certainly do 'our best'."*** They had done something similar before, and they were confident that, most likely, they can do it again using the old tactics of emotional blackmail and manipulation.

وَقَالَ لِفِتۡيَٰنِهِ ٱجۡعَلُواْ بِضَٰعَتَهُمۡ فِي رِحَالِهِمۡ لَعَلَّهُمۡ يَعۡرِفُونَهَآ
إِذَا ٱنقَلَبُوٓاْ إِلَىٰٓ أَهۡلِهِمۡ لَعَلَّهُمۡ يَرۡجِعُونَ ٦٢

Yūsuf ordered his servants to put his brothers' merchandise back into their saddlebags so that they would find it when they returned to their family, and perhaps they would come back.

In those days, trade happened mostly through bartering–the exchange of goods–than with money. The brothers had brought something with them to exchange for grain. Yūsuf told his servants to load both the grain along with the brothers' merchandise into the saddlebags. The purpose behind returning the merchandise was ***'…so that they would find it when they returned to their family, and perhaps they would come back…'*** Yūsuf was doing everything to get the brothers to come back with Binyāmīn. He had no power over them once they left, so he coaxed them through extra favours. Moreover, he knew his family was poor, and if he took their merchandise, they might not be able to return.

The question arises as to whether this was ethical for Yūsuf to do – and the response is that there is no doubt he was acting within the parameters of his power. Either the King had given him *cart blanche* authority to disperse the grain (in which case he can choose who to gift to), or else he would have reimbursed the treasury from his own money. It is inconceivable that Yūsuf would have abused his power in an unethical fashion.

فَلَمَّا رَجَعُوٓاْ إِلَىٰٓ أَبِيهِمۡ قَالُواْ يَـٰٓأَبَانَا مُنِعَ مِنَّا ٱلۡكَيۡلُ فَأَرۡسِلۡ
مَعَنَآ أَخَانَا نَكۡتَلۡ وَإِنَّا لَهُۥ لَحَـٰفِظُونَ ﴿٦٣﴾

When Yūsuf's brothers returned to their father, they pleaded, "O our father! We have been denied 'further' supplies. So send our brother with us so that we may receive our measure, and we will definitely watch over him."

The brothers hurried back to Palestine, eager to tell their story to Yaʿqūb. ***'O our father! We have been denied 'further' supplies…'*** They had barely unpacked their bags before they started to pressure Yaʿqūb about the new request. ***'… So send our brother with us so that we may receive our measure.'***

We can also assume that the family must have been in a very dire situation, hence their excitement to finally get all of this grain. With all the passion at their command and a sense of urgency in their voice, they told their father Yaʿqūb that he had to send Binyāmīn with them to receive more grain from their amazing host in Egypt. Like so many years before, they assured their father again that they will protect Binyāmīn. ***'…and we will definitely watch over him.'*** These words were identical to what they had said decades ago with regards to Yūsuf, and they must have hit Yaʿqūb like a thunderbolt.

قَالَ هَلْ ءَامَنُكُمْ عَلَيْهِ إِلَّا كَمَآ أَمِنتُكُمْ عَلَىٰٓ أَخِيهِ مِن قَبْلُ
فَٱللَّهُ خَيْرٌ حَـٰفِظًا ۖ وَهُوَ أَرْحَمُ ٱلرَّٰحِمِينَ ٦٤

He responded, "Should I trust you with him as I once trusted you with his brother 'Yūsuf'?

But 'only' Allāh is the best Protector, and He is the Most Merciful of the merciful."

The Prophet ﷺ said, 'The believer is not stung twice from the same hole.'[75] Yaʿqūb has already had this experience once before, and he did not want to repeat it with Binyāmīn. ***'Should I trust you with him as I once trusted you with his brother 'Yūsuf'?'*** His reaction showed that despite the passage of time, his love for Yūsuf had not diminished, and he considered his other sons, except for Binyāmīn, responsible for the loss of Yūsuf. For this reason, he did not want Binyāmīn to go with them. ***'...But 'only' Allāh is the best Protector, and He is the Most Merciful of the merciful.'*** Yaʿqūb turned to Allāh, beseeching Him with one of His beautiful names, *Al-Ḥāfiẓ*, the Guardian and Protector. He put his *tawakkul*, or reliance in Allāh, believing that He will protect him and his children.

We may draw some parallels between the brothers of Yūsuf and our world. The reason Yaʿqūb did not trust his sons is that their reputation was in tatters. If this is the case for this world, then how much more so for the next life? Our admission into *Jannah* will require a far better reputation and credentials.

Now the plan of Yūsuf comes into action.

---

[75] *Ṣaḥīḥ* of al-Bukhārī (6133).

وَلَمَّا فَتَحُواْ مَتَٰعَهُمۡ وَجَدُواْ بِضَٰعَتَهُمۡ رُدَّتۡ إِلَيۡهِمۡۖ قَالُواْ يَٰٓأَبَانَا
مَا نَبۡغِيۖ هَٰذِهِۦ بِضَٰعَتُنَا رُدَّتۡ إِلَيۡنَاۖ وَنَمِيرُ أَهۡلَنَا وَنَحۡفَظُ
أَخَانَا وَنَزۡدَادُ كَيۡلَ بَعِيرٖۖ ذَٰلِكَ كَيۡلٞ يَسِيرٞ ٦٥

When they opened their bags, they dis-covered that their merchandise had been returned to them. They argued, "O our father! What more can we ask for? Here is our merchandise, fully returned to us. Now we can buy more food for our family. We will watch over our brother, and obtain an extra camel-load of grain. That load can be easily secured."

'When they opened their bags, they discovered that their merchandise had been returned to them…' As mentioned earlier, returning their merchandise was part of Yūsuf's strategy to lure the brothers back with Binyāmīn. They also understood that this was not an accident and used it to make their request about Binyāmīn more forceful. ***'… They argued, "O our father! What more can we ask for? Here is our merchandise, fully returned to us…"'*** The term *mā nabghī* can have two meanings. The first is, 'What more can we desire? What more do you think we want? Here is our returned merchandise. Do you think we are trying to trick you?' The second interpretation is, 'We don't mean any evil; the only reason we want Binyāmīn to accompany us is so we can get more grain.' ***'…Now we can buy more food for our family. We will watch over our brother, and***

obtain an extra camel-load of grain. That load can be easily secured.' Yūsuf, in his wisdom, had refused to give any of the brothers more than a camel load of grain. An extra person will entitle them to receive another camel load of food supplies. This was the policy of Yūsuf: one camel's load of grain per person.

We can derive an interesting *fiqh* benefit from this part of the story. Some scholars have said that for any transaction to be valid, one must verbalize it. So, the seller must say, 'I am selling you this grain,' and the buyer must say, 'I accept this grain'. One can also write the agreement, but there must be something apparent. These scholars note that this applies to all types of commodities. But this story shows that one may also have an unspoken mutual understanding, if both parties are likely to agree.Yūsuf's implicit transaction was, 'Take this for free'. Also, we see that it is permissible to give extra merchandise to the buyer and return his money as long as it is voluntary.

قَالَ لَنْ أُرْسِلَهُۥ مَعَكُمْ حَتَّىٰ تُؤْتُونِ مَوْثِقًا مِّنَ ٱللَّهِ لَتَأْتُنَّنِى
بِهِۦٓ إِلَّآ أَن يُحَاطَ بِكُمْ ۖ فَلَمَّآ ءَاتَوْهُ مَوْثِقَهُمْ قَالَ ٱللَّهُ عَلَىٰ
مَا نَقُولُ وَكِيلٌ ٦٦

Yaʿqūb insisted, "I will not send him with you until you give me a solemn oath by Allāh that you will certainly bring him back to me, unless you are totally overpowered." Then after they had given him their oaths, he concluded, "Allāh is a Witness to what we have said."

Perhaps Yūsuf's gracious treatment of the brothers had weighed the heaviest in persuading Yaʿqūb to let Binyāmīn go. Yaʿqūb was now cautiously inclined, so he said, ***'I will not send him with you until you give me a solemn oath by Allāh that you will certainly bring him back to me...'*** He asked them to swear by Allāh, which is a very, very serious matter in our religion. Allāh says in the Qur'ān, *'Those who trade Allāh's covenant and their oaths for a fleeting gain will have no share in the Hereafter.'*[76] Yaʿqūb was a prophet, and he had taught his children about the importance of oaths in Islam, especially in the name of Allāh. He knew that they would never swear by Allāh and violate that oath. He asked them to give a solemn oath, and then said, ***'Allāh is a Witness to what we have said.'***

وَقَالَ يَٰبَنِيَّ لَا تَدْخُلُوا۟ مِنۢ بَابٍ وَٰحِدٍ وَٱدْخُلُوا۟ مِنْ أَبْوَٰبٍ
مُّتَفَرِّقَةٍ ۖ وَمَآ أُغْنِى عَنكُم مِّنَ ٱللَّهِ مِن شَىْءٍ ۖ إِنِ ٱلْحُكْمُ
إِلَّا لِلَّهِ ۖ عَلَيْهِ تَوَكَّلْتُ ۖ وَعَلَيْهِ فَلْيَتَوَكَّلِ ٱلْمُتَوَكِّلُونَ ﴿٦٧﴾

He then instructed 'them', "O my sons! Do not enter 'the city' all through one gate, but through separate gates. I cannot help

---

76 *Āl ʿImrān* (3: 77).

you against 'what is destined by' Allāh in the least. It is only Allāh Who decides. In Him, I put my trust. And in Him, let the faithful put their trust."

After the brothers swore by Allāh, Yaʿqūb let them take Binyāmīn. However, before they departed, he gave them some advice about the journey. ***'O my sons! Do not enter 'the city' all through one gate but through separate gates...'*** In ancient times, kingdoms had walls around their cities instead of borders. Walls provided security against a surprise attack, as well as a checkpoint for people coming and going. Yaʿqūb's advice that his eleven sons not enter through the same gate had mainly to do with avoiding suspicion and the evil eye. The sons would have stood out had they entered through the same gate together. A group of people walking into a strange town with a different belief, language, and customs required caution. People of the city may have felt threatened, hence Yaʿqūb's advice to his sons to enter from various gates, and then gather together inside.

The second reason was spiritual: Yaʿqūb wanted to protect them from *al-ʿayn* or the evil eye. For one man to have eleven sons was a big blessing and honour at the time. On top of that, these brothers were young, strong, and handsome. Yaʿqūb was worried that their appearance might attract the evil eye of onlookers.

What exactly is the evil eye? Is it superstition or reality? Despite some people denying it as superstition, the Qur'ān and *Sunnah* confirm the existence of the evil eye. Several hadith mention it, and there are indirect references to it in the Qur'ān. The Prophet ﷺ said in an authentic hadith, 'The evil eye is a reality.'[77] In Sūrah al-Falaq, Allāh taught us to seek protection from '*...the evil of an envier when they envy.*'[78]

The cause of the evil eye is jealousy, and it affects its victims adversely. Allāh allows it to occur when a person looks at someone's wealth, beautify, and position or something admirable with resentment because they do not have those things. Although the eye is the main culprit – hence the name 'evil eye'– the harm can also be caused by the feeling of jealousy in the heart without seeing the victim. In Islam, one should protect themselves and others from the damage of the evil eye by saying, *ma shā' Allāh*. Our Prophet ﷺ told us that, 'Envy consumes good deeds just as fire burns wood.'[79]

How do the effects of the evil eye manifest on the victim? The strongest opinion is that jealousy empowers *Shayṭān* to harm the victim. The person who inflicts the evil eye, even unintentionally, is sinful and will be held accountable for it on the Day of Judgement because they allowed their jealousy to go unchecked.

The correct way to react when we see something good in someone that we don't have is to invoke Allāh's continued blessings on them and pray for the same for themselves. The Prophet ﷺ said, 'If one of you sees

[77] *Ṣaḥīḥ* of Muslim (2188).
[78] *al-Falaq* (113: 5).
[79] *Sunan* of Ibn Mājah (4210).

something from his brother, or in himself, or in his wealth which impresses him, then supplicate for him to be blessed in it. Verily, the evil eye of envy is true.'[80] We must never wish that the other person loses their blessing.

So how do we protect ourselves against this invisible enemy? We should seek refuge with Allāh and recite Sūrah al-Falaq frequently. The Prophet ﷺ used to supplicate, 'O Allāh! I seek refuge with Your Perfect Words from every devil and poisonous pests and every evil, harmful, envious eye.'[81] We should not show off or boast about Allāh's blessings upon us. If done intentionally, it is sinful; if done unintentionally, it would cause people's jealousy. The scholars say that the best *duʿā'* is to say , *ma shā' Allāh,* 'Whatever Allāh Wills has occurred,' and *tabārak Allāh,* 'Blessed is Allāh'. We find its evidence in the story of the people of the two gardens in Sūrah al-Kahf.[82]

For the one afflicted by the evil eye, there is also a physical cure: washing with the *wuḍū'* water of the one who affected them. We know this from a hadith recorded in *Muwaṭṭa* of Imam Mālik.[83] What the hadith means is that if we know who caused the evil eye, we should ask them to perform *wuḍū'*. The one afflicted should collect the *wuḍū* water that dripped from the person's limbs and wash with it.

We strive to take precautions, but in the end, we put our trust in Allāh. As Yaʿqūb said, ***'...I cannot help you***

---

[80] *Musnad* of Aḥmad (15273).
[81] *Ṣaḥīḥ* of al-Bukhārī (590).
[82] *al-Kahf* (18: 39).
[83] *Muwaṭṭa* of Mālik (50: 1).

against 'what is destined by' Allāh in the least. It is only Allāh Who decides. In Him, I put my trust. And in Him, let the faithful put their trust.' This statement teaches us the correct understanding of *īmān* and *tawakkul*. *Tawakkul* does not mean that one sits back and says, 'If Allāh Wills, then it will happen.' *Tawakkul* means that we plan well and do the best to implement it, and then leave the results to Allāh, trusting that what He decides will be the best for us.

وَلَمَّا دَخَلُوا۟ مِنْ حَيْثُ أَمَرَهُمْ أَبُوهُم مَّا كَانَ يُغْنِى عَنْهُم مِّنَ
ٱللَّهِ مِن شَىْءٍ إِلَّا حَاجَةً فِى نَفْسِ يَعْقُوبَ قَضَىٰهَا ۚ وَإِنَّهُۥ لَذُو
عِلْمٍ لِّمَا عَلَّمْنَٰهُ وَلَٰكِنَّ أَكْثَرَ ٱلنَّاسِ لَا يَعْلَمُونَ ﴿٦٨﴾

Then when they entered as their father had instructed them, this did not help them against 'the Will of' Allāh what-soever. It was just a desire in Yaʿqūb's heart, which he satisfied. He was truly blessed with 'great' knowledge because of what We had taught him, but most people have no knowledge.

The sons obeyed their father, even though he was not with them. This tells us that, despite their past crime, they still had *īmān* and virtue. However, their adherence to Yaʿqūb's advice could not change Allāh's Decree. Allāh had already willed that a calamity would befall them, and it could not be averted. Allāh tells us that entering from different gates was ***'...a desire in Yaʿqūb's heart, which he satisfied...'*** Yaʿqūb had used his best judgement to protect his sons and ensure the safe return of Binyāmīn, but this did not change the Decree of Allāh.

'...He was truly blessed with 'great' knowledge because of what We had taught him...' There are different interpretations of this statement. Some said this refers to Yaʿqūb because Allāh had given him *ʿilm*. The way it reads, it means that Allāh was calling Himself the bestower of knowledge and Yaʿqūb, its recipient.

The second interpretation is that Allāh praised Yaʿqūb because he comprehended the knowledge given to him. It's one thing to possess the knowledge, another to understand it, and yet another to act upon it.

A third interpretation, from Ibn ʿAbbās, is that Yaʿqūb acted upon the knowledge that Allāh had given him. Having the knowledge and understanding is one level, but acting upon it is a higher level. Yaʿqūb received praise for putting God-given knowledge into action.

The final interpretation is that this phrase means that Yaʿqūb understood he could not protect his sons from the Decree of Allāh, but he still had to do everything within his power to help.

'...but most people have no knowledge.' The Qur'ān uses this phrase in several places to conclude a verse matter of factly. In the context of this story, it means that most of humanity doesn't have the blessings that Yaʿqūb had: knowledge, its understanding, and how to use it.

PART EIGHT

Binyāmīn and the Ruse

وَلَمَّا دَخَلُواْ عَلَىٰ يُوسُفَ ءَاوَىٰٓ إِلَيۡهِ أَخَاهُۖ قَالَ إِنِّيٓ أَنَا۠ أَخُوكَ
فَلَا تَبۡتَئِسۡ بِمَا كَانُواْ يَعۡمَلُونَ ٦٩

When they entered Yūsuf's presence, he called his brother 'Binyāmīn' aside, and confided 'to him', "I am indeed your brother 'Yūsuf'! So do not feel distressed about what they have been doing."

We can only imagine the joy Yūsuf must have felt at seeing his brother Binyāmīn after so many years. Some scholars say that he had divided the brothers into small groups, ostensibly to host them, so that he could get a chance to take Binyāmīn aside. At the first such opportunity, he '... ***confided 'to him', "I am indeed your brother 'Yūsuf'!"'*** With the use of Arabic *innī ana,* there is a double emphasis, 'I am your only brother; I am the one that you know.' Given Binyāmīn's young age when Yūsuf disappeared, he could not have remembered the physical appearance of his older brother. But as for what happened to Yūsuf and who may have caused his disappearance, there is no doubt Binyāmīn had heard the full story from Yaʿqūb.

Some scholars say that Yūsuf's following statement proves that the brothers were mistreating Binyāmīn: ***'...So do not feel distressed about what they have been doing.'*** The statement implies that the brothers were ridiculing and harassing Binyāmīn. He was the youngest of them and the only full brother of Yūsuf. The other ten brothers came from a different mother, and, because of their large numbers, they considered themselves an *ʿuṣbah* (group).

Yūsuf confidentially informed Binyāmīn about his plan to keep him in Egypt. Opinions vary as to why Yūsuf may have planned it this way. One view is that it was on Allāh's command, and we don't know the exact reason. And verse 76 supports this: ***'...Thus did We plan for Yūsuf'*** showing that Allāh ordered Yūsuf to do so. Another opinion is that it was to save Binyāmīn from further intimidation and ridicule. And both reasons could be simultaneously correct. Yūsuf must also now find a way around the kingdom's policy that barred foreigners from taking up permanent residence in Egypt.

فَلَمَّا جَهَّزَهُم بِجَهَازِهِمْ جَعَلَ ٱلسِّقَايَةَ فِى رَحْلِ أَخِيهِ ثُمَّ أَذَّنَ
مُؤَذِّنٌ أَيَّتُهَا ٱلْعِيرُ إِنَّكُمْ لَسَٰرِقُونَ ﴿٧٠﴾

When Yūsuf had provided them with supplies, he slipped the royal cup into his brother's bag. Then a herald cried, "O people of the caravan! You must be thieves!"

It was the second time the brothers had come to Egypt, and ***'...Yūsuf had provided them with supplies...'*** They had purchased the grain and were loading it on camels. Unbeknownst to them, Yūsuf ***'...slipped the royal cup into his brother's*** (Binyāmīn's) ***bag...'*** The word used for the 'royal cup' is *siqāyah,* which can have several meanings. One is that it was the drinking cup of the King. Another more accurate interpretation is that it was the bowl for measuring the grain. Nevertheless, it seems it was a precious bowl, perhaps made of gold, and it belonged to the King. The bowl also symbolized the King's power to give grain to the people. It would not have been difficult for Yūsuf to slip it in Binyāmīn's bag when the brothers were busy loading.

The phrase, *'...**he slipped the siqāyah...**'* is in the singular form, meaning that Yūsuf physically did this. As a high-ranking minister, Yūsuf could have ordered his servants to hide the cup, but that would have exposed the secret plan. So he took matters into his own hand.

'...Then a herald cried...' *Adhān* means 'to cry out' and 'to issue a call'. An announcer bellowed, ***'O people of the caravan! You must be thieves!'*** The brothers must have been shocked to hear the accusation, knowing they hadn't stolen anything. The scholars have trouble interpreting Yūsuf's approval of this announcement because a prophet of Allāh cannot lie. One interpretation is that Yūsuf told the crier to accuse them of being thieves because they had stolen Yūsuf from Ya'qūb and therefore were kidnappers. Another explanation is that Yūsuf used technically correct language, but the crier interpreted it as 'thief'. So he said, 'The bowl has gone missing, and the last people to receive the grain were the caravan of the Canānites.' Thus the crier used his own words for the announcement, including the word 'thieves'. By the time the crier made his call, the caravan had already become suspected of thievery. Since

Yūsuf himself did not use the words 'thief' or 'stealing,' he was not liable for it.

قَالُواْ وَأَقْبَلُواْ عَلَيْهِم مَّاذَا تَفْقِدُونَ ﴿٧١﴾

They asked, turning back to him,
"What have you lost?"

Allāh says about the brothers, ***'They asked, turning back to him…,'*** and in this, there is a psychological portrayal. They turned towards their accusers and not away from them. Thieves would have become scared and ran. But they asked, ***'What have you lost?'*** Notice they used the word 'lost' because they know they hadn't stolen anything. In essence, they were saying, 'Perhaps something went missing, and you think we stole it.'

قَالُواْ نَفْقِدُ صُوَاعَ ٱلْمَلِكِ وَلِمَن جَآءَ بِهِۦ حِمْلُ بَعِيرٍ
وَأَنَا۠ بِهِۦ زَعِيمٌ ﴿٧٢﴾

The herald 'along with the guards' replied,
"We have lost the King's measuring cup. And
whoever brings it will be awarded a camel-
load 'of grain'. I guarantee it."

The word *suwāʿ* means a vessel. When we pay *Zakat al-Fiṭr*, we give a *sāʿ* of food measured in a small container, and this phrase is similar to it. It refers to the King's measuring cup that had gone missing.

The crier announced a large reward, saying, *'...whoever brings it will be awarded a camel-load 'of grain'. I guarantee it.'* During this time of famine, food had more value than money, and a camel load of grain was a great reward.

We may derive several *fiqhi* benefits from the offer of a reward for finding the lost cup or bowl. In the *fiqh* of Islamic economics, the general rule is that one must give a specific amount of money for a particular amount of work. An example would be: 'I will pay you $10 per hour,' or, 'I will pay you $10 for this product.' Both the offer and the required labor or merchandise are specified. But there are instances where one does not know the amount of time needed to complete the task. Generally, a transaction where the amount paid is known but other factors are unkown is possibly forbidden. However, there can be exceptions, and this is one such example. One may offer 'reward money' in return for finding a lost item, or one may offer a general bid of paying someone to do something without specifying the time required for that person to do the job. In the unique circumstances of Sūrah Yūsuf, this type of transaction is permissible.

Another benefit we find from this incident is the permissibility of having guarantors; it is something akin to a bondsman. Somebody provides a guarantee, 'If this person doesn't appear, then I'm financially responsible.' Here the crier provided a guarantee: 'I will guarantee this reward.'

قَالُوا۟ تَٱللَّهِ لَقَدْ عَلِمْتُم مَّا جِئْنَا لِنُفْسِدَ فِى ٱلْأَرْضِ
وَمَا كُنَّا سَـٰرِقِينَ ٧٣

Yūsuf's brothers replied, "By Allāh! You know well that we did not come to cause trouble in the land, nor are we thieves."

The brothers began to defend themselves against the accusation, saying, ***'By Allāh!'*** The exact word used here is *tāllahi*, and it is a way to swear an oath (*qasm*) in Arabic. ***'... You know well that we did not come to cause trouble in the land, nor are we thieves.'*** They appealed to the common sense of the crier and the crowd: 'Look, we've been here before, and you've seen our mannerisms. We wouldn't do such a thing.' And the brothers were right; they had not done anything unrighteous during their visits to Egypt.

One of the words for stealing in Arabic is *fasād*, which is also used for corruption, indicating that stealing is a major vice. The Prophet ﷺ said, 'Allāh curses the thief who steals...'[84] For Allāh to declare His curse or *laʿnah* on the thief is something huge; it means He has removed this person from His Mercy. There cannot be a more frightening prospect than this. We see the seriousness of stealing reflected in the Qur'ānic punishment of the cutting off of the hand for those who meet the pre-requisites. In the sight of Allāh, the hand that steals is worthy of being removed. The thief has no honour, which is why the punishment is

---

84 *Ṣaḥīḥ* al-Bukhārī 6799.

so severe. Stealing was also a significant crime in Egyptian society.

قَالُواْ فَمَا جَزَٰٓؤُهُۥٓ إِن كُنتُمۡ كَٰذِبِينَ ٧٤

Yūsuf's men asked, "What should be the price for theft, if you are lying?"

An accusing crowd gathered around the brothers of Yūsuf, who were strangers in their land. They poignantly asked, ***'What should be the price for theft, if you are lying?'*** Meaning if it turned out that you were lying about your innocence, how should we punish you? Under Egyptian laws, no foreigner could remain in Egypt. A thief would be punished by whipping or repaying double the amount he stole. If Binyāmīn were to be found guilty, the law of the land would be enforced on him, followed by expulsion from the country. By putting the question of penalty back to the brothers, they seemed to bypass their laws.

قَالُواْ جَزَٰٓؤُهُۥ مَن وُجِدَ فِي رَحۡلِهِۦ فَهُوَ جَزَٰٓؤُهُۥۚ كَذَٰلِكَ
نَجۡزِي ٱلظَّٰلِمِينَ ٧٥

Yūsuf's brothers responded, "The price will be 'the enslavement of' the one in whose bag the cup is found. That is how we punish the wrongdoers."

Under the law of Yaʿqūb and the Children of Isrāʾīl, the penalty for theft was that the thief would become the slave of the one from whom he stole. It seems that Allāh put it in the hearts of the Egyptians to ask about the punishment under the laws of the brothers' country. Of course, Yūsuf knew that, but he could not apply Allāh's *Sharīʿah* in Egypt. Allāh created that possibility when the brothers responded to the Egyptian crowd that the punishment for stealing in their laws was ***"…'the enslavement of' the one in whose bag the cup is found. That is how we punish the wrongdoers."*** It was nothing but Allāh's plan that the matter ends this way.

فَبَدَأَ بِأَوْعِيَتِهِمْ قَبْلَ وِعَآءِ أَخِيهِ ثُمَّ ٱسْتَخْرَجَهَا مِن وِعَآءِ أَخِيهِ ۚ
كَذَٰلِكَ كِدْنَا لِيُوسُفَ ۖ مَا كَانَ لِيَأْخُذَ أَخَاهُ فِى دِينِ ٱلْمَلِكِ إِلَّآ أَن
يَشَآءَ ٱللَّهُ ۚ نَرْفَعُ دَرَجَٰتٍ مَّن نَّشَآءُ ۗ وَفَوْقَ كُلِّ ذِى عِلْمٍ عَلِيمٌ ﴿٧٦﴾

Yūsuf began searching their bags before that of his brother 'Binyāmīn', then brought it out of Binyāmīn's bag. This is how We inspired Yūsuf to plan. He could not have taken his brother under the King's law, but Allāh had so willed. We elevate in rank whoever We will. But above those ranking in knowledge is the One All-Knowing.

Up until this point, Allāh had used the plural, to represent the crowd or the mob. Now the focus changes. We move to the singular, ***'Yūsuf began...'*** Yūsuf knew what he was doing. Allāh used the word, *fabada'*, meaning Yūsuf began to take charge. He started, ***'...searching their bags...'*** He played the plot out, slowly and methodically, going through each bag. The brothers were confident that the cup would not be found in any of their bags. Despite their past crime, they were too righteous to steal. But the searcher ***'... then brought it out of Binyāmīn's bag...'***

Imagine the brothers' utter shock! Per Allāh's beautiful plan, Yūsuf was able to keep Binyāmīn with him. Allāh says that without His perfect plan ***'...He could not have taken his brother under the King's law...'*** or under the *dīn* of the *Malik*. Allāh has used the term *dīn* to refer to the King's law, even though he was a polytheist. This tells us that the word *'dīn'* does not only mean religion but that it has a broader connotation; it is a whole way of life.

'...We elevate in rank whoever We will. But above those ranking in knowledge is the One All-Knowing.' This beautiful description depicts for us how Allāh, in His perfect justice, elevates people in ranks. One of the qualities of Allāh is *rafīʿ darajāt*, the One Who Raises the Ranks, and He does so based on a person's faith and knowledge. In Sūrah al-Mujādilah, He said, *'Allāh will elevate those of you who are faithful, and 'raise' those gifted with knowledge in rank'.*[85] Yūsuf manifested both faith and knowledge. The Qur'ān repeatedly highlights the linkage between knowledge and rank.

---

[85] *al-Mujādilah* (58: 11).

The Prophet ﷺ said, 'The superiority of the scholar over the devout worshipper is like the superiority of the full moon over the rest of the heavenly bodies.'[86] Knowledge is how Allāh prefers some people over others. It is how He showed the angels that Ādam was superior. Allāh did not create Ādam bigger, stronger, or faster than the angels; Ādam was superior to them through knowledge.

قَالُوٓا۟ إِن يَسْرِقْ فَقَدْ سَرَقَ أَخٌ لَّهُۥ مِن قَبْلُ ۚ فَأَسَرَّهَا يُوسُفُ فِى نَفْسِهِۦ وَلَمْ يُبْدِهَا لَهُمْ ۚ قَالَ أَنتُمْ شَرٌّ مَّكَانًا ۖ وَٱللَّهُ أَعْلَمُ بِمَا تَصِفُونَ ﴿٧٧﴾

'To distance themselves,' Yūsuf's brothers argued, "If he has stolen, so did his 'full' brother before." But Yūsuf suppressed his outrage, revealing nothing to them and said 'to himself', "You are in such an evil position, and Allāh knows best 'the truth of' what you claim."

The brothers were adamant that they weren't thieves, but now that Binyāmīn was caught red-handed, they quickly distanced themselves from him. ***'If he has stolen, so did his 'full' brother before.'*** Without knowing, they falsely accused Yūsuf when they said his full brother had stolen also. The scholars say that accusing Yūsuf of previous

[86] *Sunan* of al-Tirmidhī (2682).

theft was either an outright lie, or an exaggerated story. Any person would have exploded with rage at their lie ***'...But Yūsuf suppressed his outrage, revealing nothing to them...'*** Yūsuf also did not reveal his identity. This stood in contrast to an earlier situation in which Yūsuf defended himself against the accusation of indecency. From this, we derive that while it is permissible for a Muslim to protect himself against false accusations, it is not obligatory to do so in every situation. There are times when silence is more beneficial.

Then he whispered to himself, ***'You are in such an evil position, and Allāh knows best 'the truth of' what you claim.'*** While they did not recognize the finance minister standing before them was Yūsuf, the latter knew full well what an ugly crime the brothers had committed against him. Hence, he subtly hints that while they accuse Binyāmīn of a particular crime, they themselves are guilty of a far worse crime: that of throwing their brother into a well and selling him into slavery.

قَالُوا۟ يَـٰٓأَيُّهَا ٱلْعَزِيزُ إِنَّ لَهُۥٓ أَبًا شَيْخًا كَبِيرًا فَخُذْ أَحَدَنَا مَكَانَهُۥٓ ۖ
إِنَّا نَرَىٰكَ مِنَ ٱلْمُحْسِنِينَ ﴿٧٨﴾

They appealed, "O Chief Minister! He has a very old father, so take one of us instead. We surely see you as one of the good-doers."

The brothers now realized they were in serious trouble. They had given a solemn pledge to their father to protect

Binyāmīn and bring him back home. The future of Binyāmīn seemed destined for slavery. Fearing the grief of their father, they earnestly pleaded for Binyāmīn's release.

'They appealed, "O Chief Minister!..."' The Arabic term the brothers used to address Yūsuf was Al-ʿAzīz, and because of this, some scholars thought that Yūsuf held the same position that belonged to his former master. Other scholars have said that Al-ʿAzīz here simply meant a 'person of honour', like, 'O Minister' or 'O Your Excellency'.

Then they appealed to Yūsuf's compassion, saying, ***'...He has a very old father...'*** Notice again how they said, '*he* has a father' and not, '*we* have a father'. There are two possible reasons for this. The first could be to earn extra sympathy, that the one detained was most needed and beloved by his father. The second was that they didn't have the same deep and sincere love for their father that Yūsuf and Binyāmīn did.

They used three adjectives: *ab* (father), *shaykh* (elder), and *kabīr* (noble) – all of them designed to invoke sympathy. He has a father who is a *shaykh,* meaning an elder leader of our tribe. Therefore, Binyāmīn is not just any person; he is the son of the leader. Another interpretation of *shaykh* is somebody of knowledge, and a third meaning is somebody of old age. All of them were equally applicable to Yaʿqūb. He was the leader of the tribe, a person of knowledge, and an old man. Then they added a title of honour for their father, calling him *kabīr*, a noble and great man.

They realized that it was unrealistic to expect that the minister will release Binyāmīn, so they tried to strike a deal: ***'...so take one of us instead...'*** They offered a prisoner swap.

Then they rested their case with Yūsuf's praise ***'...We surely see you as one of the good-doers.'*** There is no doubt Yūsuf deserved this praise, just like he did when he was in jail, and his fellow inmates had praised him with the same words. In the story of Yūsuf, the nobility of his character plays a paramount role.

قَالَ مَعَاذَ ٱللَّهِ أَن نَّأْخُذَ إِلَّا مَن وَجَدْنَا مَتَٰعَنَا عِندَهُۥٓ إِنَّآ إِذًا لَّظَٰلِمُونَ ﴿٧٩﴾

Yūsuf responded, "Allāh forbid that we should take other than the one with whom we found our property. Otherwise, we would surely be unjust."

Yūsuf said *maʿādhaAllāh* meaning 'the One whose refuge is sought is Allāh.' We first heard Yūsuf utter this word when the wife of Al-ʿAzīz tried to seduce him. Again, he did not say, *aʿūdhu billāh*, which would mean, 'I am the one seeking refuge in Allāh,' but instead he used the more powerful and precise *maʿādha Allāh* ***'... that we should take other than the one with whom we found our property...'*** In his careful choice of words, Yūsuf did not say 'the one who stole' because Binyāmīn did not steal. He used a neutral, non-judgemental phrase: *'the one with whom we found our property.'* Yūsuf's conduct shows us that even in difficult times, it is not allowed to lie. Our Prophet ﷺ never once uttered a lie. But it is permissible to use *tawrīyah,* or doublespeak, which a listener could understand differently than what the speaker intended. His brothers understood it to mean stealing, but that's not what Yūsuf meant. ***'...Otherwise, we would surely be unjust.'*** Yūsuf said it would be wrong to punish someone else for another person's crime, which meant that Binyāmīn will now stay with him in Egypt.

PART NINE

Deprived of Three Sons

فَلَمَّا ٱسْتَيْـَٔسُوا۟ مِنْهُ خَلَصُوا۟ نَجِيًّا ۖ قَالَ كَبِيرُهُمْ أَلَمْ تَعْلَمُوٓا۟ أَنَّ
أَبَاكُمْ قَدْ أَخَذَ عَلَيْكُم مَّوْثِقًا مِّنَ ٱللَّهِ وَمِن قَبْلُ مَا فَرَّطتُمْ
فِى يُوسُفَ ۖ فَلَنْ أَبْرَحَ ٱلْأَرْضَ حَتَّىٰ يَأْذَنَ لِىٓ أَبِىٓ أَوْ يَحْكُمَ
ٱللَّهُ لِى ۖ وَهُوَ خَيْرُ ٱلْحَٰكِمِينَ ﴿٨٠﴾

When they lost all hope in him, they spoke privately. The eldest of them said, "Do you not know that your father had taken a solemn oath by Allāh from you, nor how you failed him regarding Yūsuf before? So I am not leaving this land until my father allows me to, or Allāh decides for me, for He is the Best of Judges."

The Qur'ān used the term *istay'asū,* which means, ***'...they lost all hope...'*** The addition of *sīn* and *ta* in this word indicates that they tried persistently to get Binyāmīn released and then gave up. The eloquence of the Arabic language is peerless. As Allāh said at the beginning of this sūrah, *'Indeed, We have sent it down as an Arabic Qur'ān, so that you may understand.'*[87]

So, ***'...they spoke privately...'*** *Khalaṣū,* meaning they broke away, and *najīyā,* did it secretly; so they huddled together in secret to discuss the crisis. The eldest brother spoke first, and he was full of remorse. ***'Do you not know that your father had taken a solemn oath by Allāh from***

[87] *Yūsuf* (12: 2).

you, nor how you failed him regarding Yūsuf before?' He used the word *farraṭa,* which means, 'to be less than what is required.' In other words, we failed. In the opinion of some scholars, he is the same brother who had some compassion in the matter of Yūsuf years ago; he had then said, *'Do not kill Yūsuf. But if you must do something, throw him into the bottom of a well...'*[88] When Allāh described him at the beginning of the sūrah, He said, *'One of them said...'*[89] He was left unidentified. But here, Allāh says, ***'The eldest said...'*** It is so because our religion encourages hiding the faults of people. Allāh did not point him out when he did something blameworthy, but now he was saying something praiseworthy and hence deserved mention.

We see this also in the *Sunnah* of the Prophet ﷺ. Whenever someone committed a crime or did something wrong, he ﷺ would say, 'Why do some amongst you do this?' He ﷺ would never say, 'Why did *you* do this?' And he would never mention names. But on the other hand, when somebody did something good, the Prophet ﷺ would praise him by name.

The rest of the brothers already knew the answer to the eldest brother's rhetorical question: ***'Do you not know...?'*** It was they who had planned to kill Yūsuf and had changed the plan only after protest from the eldest brother. Being of the softer heart, the eldest brother was full of guilt, as if saying 'We did wrong before, we can't do it again. It would devastate our father.'

---

88 *Yūsuf* (12: 10).
89 *Yūsuf* (12: 10).

'...So I am not leaving this land until my father allows me to...' The elder brother desperately wanted to atone for the past mistake by self-exiling until Binyāmīn's matter got resolved favourably. It was a harsh punishment that he imposed upon himself, and we can understand its severity only by immersing in the mores of that time. Living in a foreign land, in today's parlance as an illegal immigrant, would subject him to discrimination, even imprisonment. Most importantly, he would live separated from his family. But he preferred that over the shame of facing his father, disgraced.

'...or Allāh decides for me...' What does he mean by Allāh's judgement? He might be referring to either a revelation to Ya'qūb, because he was a prophet, or that some calamity befalls him, such as death or sickness.

'...For He is the Best of Judges.' He knew Allāh's judgement was the best. Given his admission of the injustice he had committed against Yūsuf, the eldest brother saw redemption in sincere repentance, and, consequently, Allāh's forgiveness. These statements showed the stirrings of positive change in him. The other brothers were yet to experience a transformation.

ٱرْجِعُوٓا۟ إِلَىٰٓ أَبِيكُمْ فَقُولُوا۟ يَـٰٓأَبَانَآ إِنَّ ٱبْنَكَ سَرَقَ وَمَا شَهِدْنَآ
إِلَّا بِمَا عَلِمْنَا وَمَا كُنَّا لِلْغَيْبِ حَـٰفِظِينَ ﴿٨١﴾

Return to your father and say, "O our father!
Your son committed theft. We testify only

to what we know. We could not guard against the unforeseen.

Being the eldest and in charge, he now instructed the rest of them to go to Yaʿqūb and say, ***'Your son committed theft. We testify only to what we know…'*** What was this testimony? It could either be that Binyāmīn stole the bowl and that they were witnesses to it, or that they told the minister about the punishment for such crime in Yaʿqūb's religion.

'…We could not guard against the unforeseen.' 'We could not have possibly known the future.' Another interpretation is, 'We gave our promise to you based upon what we knew. We didn't know that our brother would commit a crime.' These seemed legitimate excuses. 'We did our best. We tried to fulfill the promise, but we couldn't predict the future.' Given the past baggage, they knew their father would not believe them, so they made a plan to strengthen their case.

وَسْـَٔلِ ٱلْقَرْيَةَ ٱلَّتِى كُنَّا فِيهَا وَٱلْعِيرَ ٱلَّتِىٓ أَقْبَلْنَا فِيهَا ۖ
وَإِنَّا لَصَـٰدِقُونَ ﴿٨٢﴾

Ask 'the people of' the land where we were and the caravan we traveled with. We are certainly telling the truth."

In other words, the brothers said, 'Look, it's not just us testifying to this. Everyone who was there knows this is what happened! If you don't believe us, ask the caravan that came back with us or send someone to the city to find out yourself.' ***'...We are certainly telling the truth.'***

Ya'qūb knew that Binyāmīn was not a thief, and even the brothers would never have thought that he would steal. But they saw with their own eyes that the search party found the King's cup in Binyāmīn's bag and, more importantly, that the latter did not try to defend himself. Binyāmīn's silence amounted to an admission of guilt in their eyes. But theirs was a case like that of the boy who falsely cried wolf, and when he finally spoke the truth, nobody believed him. They had literally cried wolf when they lied about Yūsuf some thirty years ago, and today their truth was held hostage to past.

قَالَ بَلْ سَوَّلَتْ لَكُمْ أَنفُسُكُمْ أَمْرًا ۖ فَصَبْرٌ جَمِيلٌ ۖ عَسَى ٱللَّهُ
أَن يَأْتِيَنِى بِهِمْ جَمِيعًا ۚ إِنَّهُۥ هُوَ ٱلْعَلِيمُ ٱلْحَكِيمُ ﴿٨٣﴾

He cried, "No! Your souls must have tempted you to do something 'evil'. So 'I am left with nothing but' beautiful patience! I trust Allāh will return them all to me. Surely, He 'alone' is the All-Knowing, All-Wise."

Notice the beauty of the Qur'ān and how it skips over unnecessary details: this is the Divine Style. The brothers, except for the eldest, have returned to Palestine, and Ya'qūb reacted to the tragic news. ***'He cried, "No!"'*** Again, he used *bal* in response, meaning 'No! This cannot be true!' Ya'qūb knew in his heart that his son Binyāmīn would never steal. He also knew that the brothers had lied before, so he judged them based on experience. But he did not have clear cut evidence and felt that what had transpired was beyond his understanding. So he used the same phrase as when they came to him with the story of Yūsuf, ***"...Your souls must have tempted you to do something 'evil'..."***

Ya'qūb was known to be a man of great patience. He had exhibited exemplary fortitude at the loss of Yū'sūf and here again he promised to do the same: *faṣabrun jamīl*.

'...I trust Allāh will return them all to me...' *'Asa* here means, 'I am hopeful'. Ya'qūb was optimistic that Allāh would bring Yūsuf, Binyāmīn, and the eldest son back. Despite suffering great tragedies any father would ever face, Ya'qūb had unflinching faith and trust in Allāh that He would not disappoint him. Allāh said in a *Hadith Qudsī*, 'I am as my servant thinks of Me...'[90] The lesson for us is that we should only have the best thoughts about Allāh.

The opposite is the case of the person with weak faith. He complains at the very first trial, 'O Allāh, why is this happening to me?' With more tests, his faith goes from complaints to questioning the religion and eventually disbelief. The story of Iblīs aptly highlights the danger of questioning Allāh's decision. He objected to prostrating to Ādam, saying to Allāh that he was better than someone created from clay. As a result, Iblīs became the biggest loser. At his request, Allāh extended his life until Judgement Day.

---

90 *Ṣaḥīḥ* of al-Bukhārī (7405).

Yet, Iblīs is using this time to spread corruption on earth. Believers humble themselves and draw nearer to Allāh at times of calamity because ***'...Surely, He 'alone' is the All-Knowing, All-Wise."***

وَتَوَلَّىٰ عَنْهُمْ وَقَالَ يَـٰٓأَسَفَىٰ عَلَىٰ يُوسُفَ وَٱبْيَضَّتْ عَيْنَاهُ
مِنَ ٱلْحُزْنِ فَهُوَ كَظِيمٌ ﴿٨٤﴾

He turned away from them, lamenting,
"O my sorrow over Yūsuf!" And his eyes
turned white out of the grief, he suppressed.

In his grief, Yaʿqūb turned away from his sons. Even though he loved all his children, but he had a special place for Yūsuf in his heart. In this moment of compounded grief, the only son who epitomized his agony was Yūsuf, so he quietly cried, ***'O my sorrow over Yūsuf!'*** *Yā asafa* is an Arabic expression for grief and pain. *Yā* is a word for calling someone or something, *asaf* is the grief, and *alif* is to invoke the image of this grief. So Yaʿqūb brought out the pain to his lips from the depths of his heart. The beautiful eloquence of this expression is impossible to render in the English language. It has been at least twenty-five years since Yūsuf disappeared, but his pain has not diminished. The brothers thought that by removing Yūsuf, their father's love would transfer to them, but it only served to increase Yaʿqūb's yearning for his most beloved son. What we learn from this story is that *Shayṭān* deludes us into thinking that sin will benefit us, even though, as a categorical rule Allāh has unblessed evil deeds.

Ya'qūb's sorrow and grief were such that ***'...his eyes turned white...'*** from weeping. Some scholars have interpreted this to mean that he went blind. Allāh knows best, but it doesn't appear that he factually became blind, but rather that his eyesight became weak. The word Allāh used for the condition of Ya'qūb's eyes is *ibyaḍḍat*, which means they 'became glazy and white'.

'...out of the grief he suppressed.' The word *kaẓīm* comes from *kaẓama,* which means 'to cover up or hold back'. Allāh could have said *huwa kāẓim* meaning 'he was withholding,' but He said *huwa kaẓīm,* meaning 'he was a suppressor and had already suppressed'. Just like Allāh's name *Al-Samīʿ* is not *Al-Sāmiʿ*. *Al-Sāmīʿ* means 'The One Who Hears,' but *Al-Samīʿ* is 'The One Who Hears All'. There is an emphasis on the verb. Allāh described Ya'qūb by saying, 'He had concealed, withdrawn, and protected because he didn't want to show his grief and he had been doing that for a very long time.'

Allāh praised Ya'qūb for controlling his emotions. Perfect faith in Allāh means that one does not turn to others for sympathy, but only to Him. It is, of course, human nature to turn to people for help and support, and it is not a sin to do so. But one needs to realize and firmly believe that all help comes from Allāh. Even when people want to help us, they cannot do so except with what Allāh has written for us.

In a hadith that sums up our creed, the Prophet ﷺ said to Ibn Abbās, "Young man, I will teach you some words.

Be mindful of Allāh, and He will protect you. Be mindful of Allāh, and you will find Him before you. If you ask, ask from Allāh. If you seek help, seek help from Allāh. Know that if the nations gathered together to benefit you, they would not benefit you unless Allāh has decreed it for you. And if the nations gathered together to harm you, they will not harm you unless Allāh has decreed it for you. The pens have been lifted, and the pages have dried."[91]

Yaʿqūb's *īmān* was at the level of *ihsān,* which is the highest; as for most of us, we need a shoulder to cry on, and there is nothing wrong with that. There is a difference between *asking* for a shoulder to cry on and *offering* comfort without being asked. While both are allowed, the highest level of *īmān* would be to shun the first but accept the second. In the early days of his mission, when the Prophet ﷺ felt down, his wife Khadījah comforted him. In later years, his other wives did the same.

We also see that crying does not go against the concept of *ṣabrun jamīl,* beautiful patience. Allāh describes Yaʿqūb as having 'beautiful patience', yet he cried, so much so that his eyes turned white. To cry and show emotion is human.

When our Prophet's ﷺ infant son, Ibrāhīm, died in his arms, he cried. Through tears, he ﷺ said, 'Verily, the eyes shed tears, and the heart is grieved, but we will not say anything except what is pleasing to our Lord. We are saddened by your departure, O Ibrāhīm.'[92] In the *Sīrah,* there are two or three other instances when he cried in the

[91] *Sunan* of al-Tirmidhī (2516).
[92] *Ṣaḥīḥ* of al-Bukhārī (1303).

presence of the Companions, and they were surprised: 'You cry as well, *Ya Rasūlullāh*?' They thought that this was not appropriate for him. The famous scholar al-Ḥasan al-Baṣrī was the student of many of the *Ṣaḥābah*, and when his son died, he began crying. One of his students looked at him disapprovingly because, in their culture, it was not a sign of manliness to cry. Al-Ḥasan said, 'Verily, Yaʿqūb cried, and Allāh did not rebuke him for that crying.' Yaʿqūb's crying did not diminish his status in the Eyes of Allāh.

قَالُواْ تَٱللَّهِ تَفْتَؤُاْ تَذْكُرُ يُوسُفَ حَتَّىٰ تَكُونَ حَرَضًا
أَوْ تَكُونَ مِنَ ٱلْهَٰلِكِينَ ﴿٨٥﴾

They said, "By Allāh! You will not cease to remember Yūsuf until you lose your health or 'even' your life."

The sons complained, ***'...You will not cease to remember Yūsuf...'*** They were disappointed that Yaʿqūb still loved Yūsuf with the same passion as before, even more so. Some of them expressed frustration at their father's attitude. *Ḥaraḍa* here means, 'You will ruin yourself. You will lose your mind. You will eventually perish from this grief.' They were irritated, 'We just told you about Binyāmīn and the eldest son, but you are obsessed with Yūsuf. When will you stop this?' Again, we see how Allāh tested them with the exact opposite of what they intended.

قَالَ إِنَّمَآ أَشْكُواْ بَثِّى وَحُزْنِىٓ إِلَى ٱللَّهِ وَأَعْلَمُ مِنَ ٱللَّهِ
مَا لَا تَعْلَمُونَ ﴿٨٦﴾

He replied, "I complain of my anguish and sorrow only to Allāh, and I know from Allāh what you do not know.

Ya'qūb said, ***'I complain of my anguish and sorrow only to Allāh...'*** *Baththh* is the most severe type of grief, and the word comes from the verb *batha,* which means 'to dissipate and spread out'. When a person reaches this level of sorrow, he babbles and becomes incoherent. It is as if Ya'qūb used this term to mock their assessment of him. He acknowledged that at times he did appear as if he was talking to Yūsuf, but they didn't have to listen.

Ya'qūb's example teaches us that complaining to Allāh is a sign of *īmān*. Our Prophet ﷺ did it after the people of Tā'if rejected his message and bloodied him. Complaining to Allāh means invoking His sympathy by talking about one's difficulties. After all, whose compassion and mercy should we seek, if not Allāh's? *Innama* here implies exclusivity, 'The Only Being I am complaining to is Allāh. I don't want your sympathy. I don't need anything from you.' What our religion prohibits is complaining *about* Allāh, for example, saying, 'Why are You allowing this to happen to me? It's not fair!'

'...and I know from Allāh what you do not know.' What does Ya'qūb mean here? Ya'qūb knew about Yūsuf's dream, while his other sons had no clue about it. Ya'qūb, therefore, knew that Yūsuf had to be alive; how else would the prophecy in the dream come to pass? What Ya'qūb may not have known was where and in what situation Yūsuf was.

يَٰبَنِيَّ ٱذْهَبُوا۟ فَتَحَسَّسُوا۟ مِن يُوسُفَ وَأَخِيهِ وَلَا تَا۟يْـَٔسُوا۟ مِن رَّوْحِ ٱللَّهِ ۖ إِنَّهُۥ لَا يَا۟يْـَٔسُ مِن رَّوْحِ ٱللَّهِ إِلَّا ٱلْقَوْمُ ٱلْكَٰفِرُونَ ﴿٨٧﴾

O my sons! Go and search 'diligently' for Yūsuf and his brother. And do not lose hope in the Mercy of Allāh, for no one loses hope in Allāh's Mercy except those with no faith."

That is why Ya'qūb told the remaining sons to go and search for their brothers and bring them back. He used the word *taḥassasū,* meaning, 'use all your senses' to find them. In other words: do whatever you can. ***'…And do not lose hope in the Mercy of Allāh, for no one loses hope in Allāh's Mercy except those with no faith.'*** He explicitly told them never to lose hope in Allāh. In this verse, Ya'qūb equated the absence of hope in Allāh with *kufr* or disbelief. A true believer must never despair of Allāh's Mercy. The word *Rawḥ* used here means 'Allāh's Mercy,' and comes from the same root as *ruḥ*. *Rawḥ* gives us comfort against stress, whereas *ruḥ* gives us life.

PART TEN

Yūsuf Reveals His Identity

فَلَمَّا دَخَلُوا۟ عَلَيْهِ قَالُوا۟ يَـٰٓأَيُّهَا ٱلْعَزِيزُ مَسَّنَا وَأَهْلَنَا ٱلضُّرُّ
وَجِئْنَا بِبِضَـٰعَةٍ مُّزْجَىٰةٍ فَأَوْفِ لَنَا ٱلْكَيْلَ وَتَصَدَّقْ عَلَيْنَآ ۖ
إِنَّ ٱللَّهَ يَجْزِى ٱلْمُتَصَدِّقِينَ ﴿٨٨﴾

When they entered Yūsuf's presence, they pleaded, "O Chief Minister! We and our family have been touched with hardship, and we have brought only scant merchandise, but 'please' give us our supplies in full and be charitable to us. Indeed, Allāh rewards the charitable."

The brothers now travelled to Egypt for the third time. Their number this time was nine, as the eldest had stayed back in Egypt. They had lived through nearly seven years of drought, and the resulting poverty had greatly distressed them. So ***'...they pleaded, "O Chief Minister! We and our family have been touched with hardship..."'*** They appealed to Yūsuf using the term *massana,* meaning that severe economic difficulties had touched them.

'...we have brought only scant merchandise...' The brothers referred to their goods as *muzjāt*, something that is second-rate and poor in quality. They were ashamed of what they had to offer, and they appealed to Yūsuf to show compassion. In a sense, they said, 'We are not beggars. We've brought something to barter, but it is not good quality.' ***'...'please' give us our supplies in full and be charitable to us...'*** The brothers wanted full measure, even extra, for their second-rate merchandise, and hence their appeal to Yūsuf's generosity. They concluded their request with the reminder that ***'...Indeed, Allāh rewards the charitable.'*** The irony of their statement could not have missed Yūsuf, for none needed a reminder of charity and God-consciousness more than they.

قَالَ هَلْ عَلِمْتُم مَّا فَعَلْتُم بِيُوسُفَ وَأَخِيهِ إِذْ أَنتُمْ جَٰهِلُونَ ﴿٨٩﴾

He asked, "Do you remember what you did to Yūsuf and his brother in your ignorance?"

Yūsuf chose this moment to reveal his identity to his brothers, saying, ***'Do you remember what you did to Yūsuf and his brother...'*** Imagine their shock at the minister's mention of Yūsuf! How in the world could the minister have known about their long lost brother and what happened to him? Wasn't it the brothers' tightly guarded secret?

Yūsuf used the third person to refer to himself to minimize their guilty feeling. And he also used ***'...in your ignorance?'***, gracefully giving them a face-saving opportunity. Despite possessing power and having every justification for despising them, Yūsuf did not criticize them directly. This exemplified the perfection of Yūsuf and his character.

The question arises: Why did Yūsuf reveal himself at this stage? Why so late, and why not before? There are two possible scenarios. The first is that Allāh told him to do so now. The prophets wait for Allāh's command.

The Prophet Muhammad ﷺ did not migrate to Madinah until Allāh permitted him.

The second scenario is that there was a practical reason. Some early books of *tafsīr* said that when Yūsuf came to power, the King at the time was the elder of the family. But now, several years later, that king had died, and his younger son had ascended the throne. Because of the young age of the new King, the senior ministers had assumed more power than the King. Being a veteran, Yūsuf had the authority to make his own decisions. The story in the Old Testament supports this explanation. By now, Yūsuf could tell the King, 'I want my family to come.'

قَالُوٓا۟ أَءِنَّكَ لَأَنتَ يُوسُفُ ۖ قَالَ أَنَا۠ يُوسُفُ وَهَٰذَآ أَخِى ۖ قَدْ مَنَّ ٱللَّهُ
عَلَيْنَآ ۖ إِنَّهُۥ مَن يَتَّقِ وَيَصْبِرْ فَإِنَّ ٱللَّهَ لَا يُضِيعُ أَجْرَ ٱلْمُحْسِنِينَ ﴿٩٠﴾

They replied 'in shock', "Are you really Yūsuf?" He said, "I am Yūsuf, and here is my brother 'Binyāmīn'! Allāh has truly been gracious to us. Surely whoever is mindful 'of Allāh' and patient, then certainly Allāh never discounts the reward of the good-doers."

The brothers were stunned. ***'They replied 'in shock', "Are you really Yūsuf?"'*** The Arabic used here is beautifully eloquent. In English, it would be like saying, 'Are you really, *really*, *that* Yūsuf?' There is a triple emphasis that we cannot translate in English. They knew that it was him, but they could hardly believe it.

'He said, "I am Yūsuf, and here is my brother 'Binyāmīn'!"' He called Binyāmīn into the court then said, ***'…Allāh has truly been gracious to us…'*** Yūsuf immediately attributed all good to Allāh. 'None of this that you see is from my power. I'm not gloating that I have the upper hand. I am not showing you who is richer and more powerful. Allāh has given us all of this.' *Manna* is a gift that is not even earned or deserved, but something that Allāh bestows because of His generosity.

'…Surely whoever is mindful 'of Allāh' and patient, then certainly Allāh never discounts the reward of the good-doers.' Notice that first, Yūsuf ascribed the blessings directly to himself from Allāh: *'Allāh has truly been gracious to us.'* Now he used the third person, *'whoever is mindful…'* He didn't say, 'I was righteous and patient, so Allāh rewarded me.' Every single word that Yūsuf used shows us over and over again, his level of humility. We could not have thought of humbler words to say on this occasion.

Yūsuf mentioned *ṣabr* because it was patience that allowed him, by the Will of Allāh, to remain in the well, then as a slave, and in prison until finally, Allāh rewarded him with ministership. He mentioned *taqwā* as well because it and *ṣabr* have been two pillars of Islamic belief and character throughout the story of Yūsuf. We can summarize the message of Sūrah Yūsuf in these words: whoever is mindful and patient will be rewarded by Allāh.

This message was equally applicable to the brothers as if Yūsuf was telling them: 'You tried to get what you wanted by disobeying Allāh, which is why you didn't get it. As for me, I was patient and put my trust in Allāh, and He gave me more than anyone could imagine.' Yūsuf sincerely sought to bring his brothers closer to Allāh. Reformation, not revenge, is always paramount on the minds of the righteous believers.

قَالُواْ تَٱللَّهِ لَقَدْ ءَاثَرَكَ ٱللَّهُ عَلَيْنَا وَإِن كُنَّا لَخَٰطِـِٔينَ ﴿٩١﴾

They admitted, "By Allāh! Allāh has truly preferred you over us, and we have surely been sinful."

Yūsuf's advice had the desired effect, and the brothers admitted to their faults: ***'By Allāh! Allāh has truly preferred you over us, and we have surely been sinful.'*** The Arabic, *wa in* is for emphasis on their admission of guilt. *Tallāhi* is an Arabic expression for an oath; the brothers swore by Allāh that they were in the wrong. They had taken the first step towards repentance.

قَالَ لَا تَثْرِيبَ عَلَيْكُمُ ٱلْيَوْمَ ۖ يَغْفِرُ ٱللَّهُ لَكُمْ ۖ وَهُوَ أَرْحَمُ ٱلرَّٰحِمِينَ ﴿٩٢﴾

Yūsuf said, "There is no blame on you today. Allāh will forgive you! He is the Most Merciful of the merciful!

The word *tathrīb* means to be reminded of one's sins and feel guilty. ***'There is no blame on you today...'*** Yūsuf did not even say, 'I will not blame you'. He said this in the third person and removed himself entirely from the picture. 'There is no blame on you,' is generic and completely neutral. ***'...Allāh will forgive you! He is the Most Merciful of the merciful!'*** The question arises: How can Yūsuf say, 'Allāh will forgive you?' What right did he have to say this? There are two responses to this question.

The first is that because the *ẓulm,* or injustice, was done to Yūsuf, but he forgave them, Allāh will also forgive. In Islam, crimes committed against fellow humans require the forgiveness of the wronged. Should the oppressor not take care of the wrong in this life, Allāh will settle the matter in the Hereafter. On the Day of Judgement, Allāh will establish justice even among animals. Therefore, one should be extra careful not to wrong others, because while Allāh may forgive sins committed against Him, He will not forgive crimes against a person unless the victim forgave. It is easier to attain Allāh's forgiveness than of people's, because He is the Most Merciful.

The second interpretation is that 'I hope that Allāh will forgive you.' Both of these interpretations are valid, and there is no contradiction between the two.

We should remember that Allāh revealed Sūrah Yūsuf when our Prophet ﷺ was undergoing the most challenging period of his life, known as the Year of Sorrow. It was the year Abū Ṭālib and Khadījah died, and he suffered violent rejection in Ṭā'if. Allāh revealed Sūrah Yūsuf to lift his spirits and cheer him up. At the pinnacle of his ﷺ

prophetic mission, when he ﷺ finally conquered Makkah, whose people had forced him to leave, he ﷺ recited this verse from Sūrah Yūsuf. He ﷺ stood at the Kaʿbah and asked the nervous people who had gathered around him, 'O Quraysh, how do you think I should treat you?' The Quraysh said, 'O Prophet of Allāh. We expect nothing but good from you.' He ﷺ then forgave them saying, 'I will only say to you what Yūsuf said to his brothers, *'There is no blame on you today.'* Go for you are unbound.'[93] Sūrah Yūsuf provided the Prophet ﷺ hope and guidance for treating the Quraysh after the Conquest of Makkah.

ٱذْهَبُوا۟ بِقَمِيصِى هَٰذَا فَأَلْقُوهُ عَلَىٰ وَجْهِ أَبِى يَأْتِ بَصِيرًا
وَأْتُونِى بِأَهْلِكُمْ أَجْمَعِينَ ﴿٩٣﴾

Go with this shirt of mine and cast it over my father's face, and he will regain his sight. Then come back to me with your whole family."

The shirt plays a recurrent role in the story of Yūsuf. The first time when the brothers brought the blood-stained shirt of Yūsuf, claiming that a wolf had attacked him; the second time, when the wife of Al-ʿAzīz tore his shirt from the back as he tried to run away from her advances; and the third time now. This time, the shirt returned as a healer.

[93] *Kitāb aṭ-Tabaqāt al-Kabīr* Ibn Saʿd.

Yūsuf told the brothers to put his shirt on Ya'qūb's face, and it will restore his vision. Also, on its final appearance, the shirt informed Ya'qūb, even before it had arrived in his presence, that Yūsuf was alive because he smelled the fragrance of his most beloved son.

After pardoning the brothers, Yūsuf invited them to bring Ya'qūb, and their families to live a comfortable life in Egypt ***'...Then come back to me with your whole family.'***

PART ELEVEN

The Dream Fulfilled

وَلَمَّا فَصَلَتِ ٱلْعِيرُ قَالَ أَبُوهُمْ إِنِّى لَأَجِدُ رِيحَ يُوسُفَ ۖ
لَوْلَآ أَن تُفَنِّدُونِ ﴿٩٤﴾

When the caravan departed 'from Egypt', their father said 'to those around him', "You may think I am senile, but I certainly sense the smell of Yūsuf."

The caravan set out on its last journey back to Palestine, bringing with it the promise of a new future. Nestled amongst the grain sacks and merchandise was the shirt of Yūsuf. Although he was hundreds of miles away, Ya'qūb could sense that his beloved son was close. He said, ***'You may think I am senile, but I certainly sense the smell of Yūsuf.'*** We saw earlier in the story that Ya'qūb had *firāsah*, a spiritual intuition that helped him understand things instinctively. Allāh had given him a sign that something was about to happen.

قَالُوا۟ تَٱللَّهِ إِنَّكَ لَفِى ضَلَٰلِكَ ٱلْقَدِيمِ ﴿٩٥﴾

They replied, "By Allāh! You are definitely still in your old delusion."

Ya'qūb anticipated that his family would think of him as insane for saying such a thing, but in his heart, he knew it was true. Some scholars say that it was his grandchildren who uttered the harsh words in reply, ***'By Allāh! You are definitely still in your old delusion.'*** But they were mistaken.

فَلَمَّآ أَن جَآءَ ٱلْبَشِيرُ أَلْقَىٰهُ عَلَىٰ وَجْهِهِۦ فَٱرْتَدَّ بَصِيرًا ۖ قَالَ أَلَمْ
أَقُل لَّكُمْ إِنِّىٓ أَعْلَمُ مِنَ ٱللَّهِ مَا لَا تَعْلَمُونَ ﴿٩٦﴾

But when the bearer of the good news arrived, he cast the shirt over Yaʿqūb's face, so he regained his sight. Yaʿqūb then said 'to his children', "Did I not tell you that I truly know from Allāh what you do not know?"

Many scholars say that the ***'...bearer of the good news...'***, the *bashīr* who carried Yūsuf's shirt, was the same son who had brought the bloody shirt to Yaʿqūb at the beginning of the story. Notice that Allāh chose to mention the good news and ignore the bad. It is a repeated theme throughout this sūrah and the Qur'ān. When praise is due, Allāh specifically mentions it, but when criticism is warranted, He tries to conceal. Imagine how this son must have felt bringing the shirt that announced Yūsuf was alive, knowing it is he who had carried the bloodied shirt to his father many years ago that caused him lasting grief.

'...he cast the shirt over Yaʿqūb's face, so he regained his sight...' With the touch of the shirt, Yaʿqūb's vision came back. Joyous at the news that Yūsuf, his most beloved son, was alive, he said, ***'Did I not tell you that I truly***

know from Allāh what you do not know?' Through all these years of separation, Ya'qūb had not lost hope about Yūsuf's eventual return. Today, Allāh had vindicated him.

قَالُوا۟ يَـٰٓأَبَانَا ٱسْتَغْفِرْ لَنَا ذُنُوبَنَآ إِنَّا كُنَّا خَـٰطِـِٔينَ ﴿٩٧﴾

They begged, "O our father! Pray for the forgiveness of our sins. We have certainly been sinful."

Finally, the brothers asked their father for forgiveness, saying, ***'We have certainly been sinful.'*** Before this, they had implored Yūsuf to forgive them; they were sincerely repentant. The first step for repentance is always the admission of guilt. One cannot repent without acknowledging they have done wrong. That's why the Prophet ﷺ said, 'Regret is part of repentance.'[94]

قَالَ سَوْفَ أَسْتَغْفِرُ لَكُمْ رَبِّىٓ ۖ إِنَّهُۥ هُوَ ٱلْغَفُورُ ٱلرَّحِيمُ ﴿٩٨﴾

He said, "I will pray to my Lord for your forgiveness. He 'alone' is indeed the All-Forgiving, Most Merciful."

Ya'qūb agreed that he would ask Allāh to forgive his sons, but his use of the term, ***'I will...'***, clearly indicated but

[94] *Sunan* of Ibn Mājah (4252).

'not right now'. Why did Yaʿqūb delay seeking Allāh's forgiveness for his repentant sons? Most Muslim scholars said that Yaʿqūb wanted to delay the *duʿā'* until the last third of the night, for his *tahajjud* prayer, because of the high status of this prayer with Allāh. The Prophet ﷺ said, 'The Lord descends every night to the lowest heaven when one-third of the night remains and says: "Who will call upon Me, that I may answer Him? Who will ask of Me, that I may give him? Who will seek My forgiveness, that I may forgive him?"'[95] Yaʿqūb wanted to be in *sajdah* during the most blessed time when he asked his Lord's forgiveness for his sons.

In Islam, a person's final status is dependent upon how they ended their life, not on how they began it. That is why we should pray for *ḥusn al-khitām*, a good end. While the brothers started wrong, they were about to end on a positive note. The concept of last actions determining a person's status in our religion holds out hope even for the worst sinner. A modern court of law would have charged the brothers with the attempted murder of a child, but Allāh gave them a chance to repent. Not only were they forgiven, but, according to the majority opinion, they became minor prophets. That is why the dream compared them to the stars and their parents to the sun and the moon. The story of Yūsuf reminds us that the gates of Allāh's mercy are wide open and that we should seek forgiveness without delay, knowing that He does not accept repentance from a person who is in the pangs of death. If Allāh could forgive

[95] *Ṣaḥīḥ* of al-Bukhārī (1145).

them and make them prophets after the commission of a major crime, then surely there is hope for us.

فَلَمَّا دَخَلُوا۟ عَلَىٰ يُوسُفَ ءَاوَىٰٓ إِلَيْهِ أَبَوَيْهِ وَقَالَ ٱدْخُلُوا۟ مِصْرَ إِن شَآءَ ٱللَّهُ ءَامِنِينَ ﴿٩٩﴾

When they entered Yūsuf's presence, he received his parents 'graciously' and said, "Enter Egypt, Allāh willing, in security."

The brothers embarked on their fourth journey to Egypt, but this time they had their parents, wives, and children with them. Also, this was not the journey of a traveller; now, they were emigrants to Egypt at Yūsuf's invitation. Their number was around seventy, and they had their worldly possessions with them. In the history of the Jewish people, the Children of Isrā'īl will return to Palestine five centuries later, known as the Exodus, under the Prophet Mūsa.

The scholars say that Yūsuf led a home-coming procession to the outskirts of the city to greet his family with fanfare ***'...he received his parents 'graciously'...'*** For Ya'qūb, it was the first visit to Egypt. Allāh had promised Ya'qūb Palestine, but he had never cultivated it. He lived in the wilderness in a barren valley as a Bedouin. When the drought struck, people began dying, and life became tough. He was now an old man and looked forward to a safe and peaceful new life with his most beloved son and other family members. Such a reunion indeed deserved a celebration and thanks.

Yūsuf said, ***'Enter Egypt, Allāh willing, in security.'*** In promising safe resettlement in Egypt, Yūsuf reminded them that Allāh alone was the source of their safety and prosperity in the new land and that he was just a means.

وَرَفَعَ أَبَوَيْهِ عَلَى ٱلْعَرْشِ وَخَرُّواْ لَهُۥ سُجَّدًاۖ وَقَالَ يَـٰٓأَبَتِ هَـٰذَا تَأْوِيلُ
رُءْيَـٰىَ مِن قَبْلُ قَدْ جَعَلَهَا رَبِّى حَقًّاۖ وَقَدْ أَحْسَنَ بِىٓ إِذْ أَخْرَجَنِى مِنَ
ٱلسِّجْنِ وَجَآءَ بِكُم مِّنَ ٱلْبَدْوِ مِنۢ بَعْدِ أَن نَّزَغَ ٱلشَّيْطَـٰنُ بَيْنِى
وَبَيْنَ إِخْوَتِىٓۚ إِنَّ رَبِّى لَطِيفٌ لِّمَا يَشَآءُۚ إِنَّهُۥ هُوَ ٱلْعَلِيمُ ٱلْحَكِيمُ ﴿١٠٠﴾

Then he raised his parents to the throne, and they all fell down in prostration to Yūsuf, who then said, "O my dear father! This is the interpretation of my old dream. My Lord has made it come true. He was truly kind to me when He freed me from prison, and brought you all from the desert after Shayṭān had ignited rivalry between my siblings and me. Indeed, my Lord is Subtle in fulfilling what He wills. Surely, He 'alone' is the All-Knowing, All-Wise."

Yūsuf then ***'...raised his parents to the throne...'*** It is not clear which throne Allāh means here. Did Yūsuf have a throne? Or did he symbolically put his parents on the throne of Egypt to show them respect? In either case, it was an esteemed finale to a life that originated in the barren lands of Palestine.

Yūsuf's parents came off the throne and ***'...fell down in prostration ...'*** in front of him, as did the brothers. Some scholars said they fell onto their faces, and others said they bowed down in *rukūʿ*. The meaning of *sujjada* in Arabic can have both definitions.

We must mention here that Yaʿqūb's *Sharīʿah* allowed lowering of the head as a sign of respect, but in our *Sharīʿah* it is forbidden. Allāh has modified the laws of previous prophets over time, and the law of our Prophet ﷺ is the most perfect. It is not permitted for us to bow our heads to any creature to show respect; it is reserved only for Allāh. A hadith says that the Companion Muʿādh ibn Jabal entered the Prophet's *masjid* upon return from Syria and fell in front of the Prophet ﷺ in *sajdah*. The Prophet ﷺ was shocked and said, 'What is this, O Muʿādh?' Muʿādh replied, 'I went to Shām and saw them prostrating to their bishops and patricians, and I wanted to do that for you, as you are more deserving than they are.' The Prophet ﷺ said, 'Do not do that!'[96]

The above verse mentions that Yūsuf put his 'parents' on the throne, even though Yaʿqūb's wife was Yūsuf's maternal aunt, not his biological mother, who had died long ago. Allāh tells us that a mother's sister has the same rights as a mother, hence it is allowed to address her as 'mother'. Our Prophet ﷺ confirmed this. In love, a *khāla* is more like a mother than the father's sister, even though both are close relatives.

---

[96] *Sunan* of Ibn Mājah (1853).

'O my dear father! This is the interpretation of my old dream.' The word *tā'wīl* here means 'actualization'. Yūsuf was saying, it has been years since I saw that dream, but now Allāh has fulfilled it. ***'My Lord has made it come true.'*** The dreams of the prophets are a type of revelation. Yūsuf immediately ascribed the blessings to Allāh, ***'He was truly kind to me when He freed me from prison and brought you all from the desert after Shayṭān had ignited rivalry between my siblings and me...'*** He used amazingly eloquent phrases, look 'how generous Allāh has been to me that He caused me to leave the prison'. Notice he did not mention the well, even though to be saved from the well was a bigger blessing. He would have died in the well, but he was not going to die in prison. In his exceptional graciousness, Yūsuf deliberately omitted the well because mentioning it would have embarrassed the brothers. Notice also that he blamed *Shayṭān* for his brothers' evil actions.

'Indeed, my Lord is Subtle in fulfilling what He wills.' Yūsuf chose *Al-Laṭīf* to refer to Allāh. *Al-Laṭīf* means 'the One who is Aware of the most intricate and hidden secrets, or *ghayb*.' There is also a secondary meaning that Allāh is kind. He knows us intimately and provides protective and nurturing care for us, despite our shortcomings and faults.

'Surely, He 'alone' is the All-Knowing, All-Wise.' Allāh is *Al-ʿAlīm* and *Al-Ḥakīm*. He knows everything and is All-Wise. These two names of Allāh are very relevant here. Allāh knew all along what will happen, and it was His Plan. Neither Yūsuf nor his family knew what future awaited them.

رَبِّ قَدْ ءَاتَيْتَنِى مِنَ ٱلْمُلْكِ وَعَلَّمْتَنِى مِن تَأْوِيلِ ٱلْأَحَادِيثِ ۚ فَاطِرَ
ٱلسَّمَٰوَٰتِ وَٱلْأَرْضِ أَنتَ وَلِىِّۦ فِى ٱلدُّنْيَا وَٱلْءَاخِرَةِ ۖ تَوَفَّنِى مُسْلِمًا
وَأَلْحِقْنِى بِٱلصَّٰلِحِينَ ﴿١٠١﴾

"My Lord! You have surely granted me (something of) authority and taught me the interpretation of dreams. 'O' Originator of the heavens and the earth! You are my Guardian in this world and the Hereafter. Allow me to die as one who submits and join me with the righteous."

'My Lord...' literally, *'O my Rabb'*. *Ar-Rabb* has three meanings. The first is the Owner; the second is Nourisher and Sustainer; and the third is Lord and Master. All of these meanings are in display here.

Yūsuf now said, ***'You have surely granted me (something of) authority and taught me the interpretation of dreams.'*** In saying this, Yūsuf invoked two names of Allāh, *Al-Mālik,* the Owner of Dominion, and *Al-'Alīm*, the All-Knowing. Allāh had given him authority in a small, worldly kingdom, and from His infinite knowledge, He had taught Yūsuf the interpretation of dreams. Yūsuf said "'something of' authority", which meant that a finance minister's authority was minuscule compared to the power of Allāh and that his ability to interpret dreams was minimal compared to the knowledge of Allāh.

Allāh chooses prophets from the best among His creation, who generally personify spirituality and knowledge, not worldly power. In Yūsuf's case, he also wielded earthly authority. And to the Prophet Sulaymān, Allāh gave the unmatched kingdom of this world. Our Prophet ﷺ was without doubt one of the most successful of Allāh's messengers: he combined *al-mulk* and *al-ʿilm*. He was not a prophet-king, but he possessed political authority as the head of a fully functioning state, and the spiritual power as the prophet of Allāh.

Yūsuf began his *duʿā'* by acknowledging Allāh's blessings on him. He did this for several reasons. One of the best ways to show gratitude to Allāh is to mention His favour. Thanking Allāh for His favours will lead to more blessings. As Allāh said, *'If you are grateful, I will increase you in favour.'*[97]

Another possible reason could be that Yūsuf wanted to acknowledge that Allāh was not just generous, but He was *Al-Akram*, the Most Generous. Yūsuf knew that the best way to supplicate to Allāh was to preface it with thanks and praise.

"'O' Originator of the heavens and the earth!" After calling Allāh by *Ar-Rabb*, Yūsuf now mentioned another name of Allāh: *Al-Fāṭir*, the Originator. In the Qur'ān, what follows this name is *al-samāwāti wa-l-arḍ*, the heavens and the earth. *Al-Fāṭir* can be used only for Allāh because He is the only one who can create things out of nothing. He originates creation, not just changes the shape of things. As for humans, we only modify what Allāh has already created.

---

97 *al-Ibrahīm* (14:7).

'You are my Guardian in this world and the Hereafter.' Yūsuf used another of Allāh's name: *Al-Walī,* which could mean protector and friend. *Al-Mawla* and *Al-Walī* are two names of Allāh with similar meanings because they come from the same root, *yali,* which means to be next to someone or something. *Al-Walī,* therefore, means someone close. In Arabic, one's supporters, family, and protectors are called *walī.* The Qur'ān describes Allāh as the *walī* of believers and orphans. In the case of a woman, a *walī* is her guardian.

Another connotation for *Al-Fāṭir* and *Al-Walī* appearing together is that *Al-Fāṭir* is the Originator and Creator of the physical world, and *Al-Walī* is our guide and protector in the spiritual realm. He has created us physically, and He will nourish us spiritually. It is as if Yūsuf was saying, 'I know, O Allāh, that You created not just me, but this whole existence, from nothing. And I know that all of this happened because of You, You were protecting me, and You had a plan. You are my *Walī* in this world and the next.'

After displaying proper manners for *duʿā,* Yūsuf presented his request: ***'Allow me to die as one who submits...'*** His supplication is so profound. He first acknowledged all of Allāh's blessings upon him, but now he wanted something more precious: to die in a state of Islam. We should reflect deeply on this point, because in the end, what matters most is that we meet Allāh while submitting to Him.

Next, he asked, ***'...and join me with the righteous.'*** It, too, is very profound. Yūsuf begged Allāh to resurrect him in the next life with the righteous. He wanted to be in the most distinguished group of people. This highlights the importance of seeking good companionship. The Prophet

ﷺ said, 'A man is upon the religion of his best friend, so let one of you look at whom he befriends.'[98] A person generally copies the behavior of those close to him. Therefore, the righteous and their righteous friends of this world will be brought together in the Hereafter.

Aisha, the wife of the Prophet ﷺ, reported that moments before his soul departed, he ﷺ prayed to Allāh to join him "With those on whom You have bestowed Your Grace, with the prophets and the truthful, the martyrs and the good-doers. O Allāh, forgive me and have mercy upon me and join me with the Companionship on high." It was as if he was trying to recite what Allāh had revealed in the Qur'ān about the righteous people: *"And whoever obeys Allāh and the Messenger, then they will be in the company of those on whom Allāh has bestowed His grace, of the prophets, the truthful, the martyrs, and the righteous. And how excellent are these companions!"*[99]

According to history books, Ya'qūb died only two or three years after migrating to Egypt. Yūsuf was grief-stricken, and Allāh willed that he dies shortly after his father. In that context, this *du'ā'* becomes even more profound. No doubt, the most righteous person at that time was Yūsuf's father. In these brief words, with the most profound meaning, Yūsuf affirmed *tawḥīd*, the perfection of Allāh's names and attributes, and his sincere submission to Allāh. And with this comprehensive *du'ā'*, the story of Yūsuf came to a perfect conclusion.

---

98 *Sunan* of al-Tirmidhī (2378).

99 *al-Nisā* (4:69).

PART TWELVE

Reminders to the Prophet ﷺ

ذَٰلِكَ مِنْ أَنۢبَآءِ ٱلْغَيْبِ نُوحِيهِ إِلَيْكَ ۖ وَمَا كُنتَ لَدَيْهِمْ إِذْ أَجْمَعُوٓا۟
أَمْرَهُمْ وَهُمْ يَمْكُرُونَ ﴿١٠٢﴾

That is from the stories of the unseen which We reveal to you 'O Prophet'. You were not present when they 'all' made up their minds, and when they plotted 'against Yūsuf'.

With the conclusion of the story of Yūsuf, the focus now turns back to our Prophet ﷺ. Allāh says, ***'That is from the stories of the unseen which We reveal to you...'*** He used the term *dhālik,* which serves to elevate the story. The difference between *hādha* and *dhālik* is distance: *hādha* is here, and *dhālik* is over there. Technically, *hādha* would be more appropriate because it refers to a story that has just concluded, but by using *dhālik,* Allāh wants to indicate its superiority over other stories.

'...You were not present when they 'all' made up their minds and when they plotted 'against Yūsuf'.' Allāh mentions just one incident from a long story to underline the fact that the Prophet ﷺ was not there when the brothers hatched their secret plot. Why doesn't Allāh highlight any other aspect of the story? He didn't say that the Prophet ﷺ was not with them when they were in the palace of the king, or that the Prophet ﷺ was not with Yūsuf when he was at the bottom of the well. It is because the plotting is the most secret part of the story; no-one else knew about it. Nobody could have known about this conversation other than Allāh. From *'You were not present'* it appears that Allāh has addressed only our Prophet ﷺ, but the fact is that the entire humanity is the addressee. The statement was also a reminder to the people of Makkah that the Qur'ān is a Divine Revelation.

The greatest miracle Allāh gave to our Prophet ﷺ is the Qur'ān, and the stories of ancient societies in it are proof that it is from the Divine. Arabia was not a civilized society. Makkah was a city of a thousand people, and only around ten people knew how to read and write. There were no books or Jewish and Christian communities living amongst them who could tell them stories from their scriptures. A century ago, some people had alleged that the Prophet ﷺ had copied the ancient stories from the Bible. However, the first Arabic translation of the Bible wasn't available until around 180 AH, several generations after the passing of the Prophet ﷺ. No serious researcher can defend this spurious theory, knowing there are so many differences in each version of the Bible. Many of the details of the story of Yūsuf do not exist in the Old Testament; we only find them in the Qur'ān. So, where did the Prophet ﷺ get the story of Yūsuf? The only logical answer is that he learned it from Revelation. There is no way the Prophet ﷺ could have narrated the story in fine detail and with impeccable accuracy, highlighting even the most secretive plots, had Allāh not informed him about it.

وَمَآ أَكۡثَرُ ٱلنَّاسِ وَلَوۡ حَرَصۡتَ بِمُؤۡمِنِينَ ١٠٣

And most people will not believe,
no matter how keen you are.

Allāh concluded the story of Yūsuf by talking about its miraculous aspects, then comforted the Prophet ﷺ with the words, *'**And most people will not believe, no matter how keen you are.**'* The word *ḥarasta* means keen, zealous, or anxious, and it was the quality of our Prophet ﷺ. He was always extra eager and passionate about spreading the message of Islam. Allāh used this word for our Prophet ﷺ in Sūrah Tawbah as well, *'There certainly has come to you a messenger from among yourselves. He is concerned about your suffering, anxious for your well-being, and gracious and merciful to the believers.'*[100] He ﷺ sincerely wanted guidance for his people.

This verse makes it clear that most of humanity will not believe, no matter how much a prophet tried. Many of us have a very naïve understanding of *daʿwah*. We think that with a few pieces of evidence, we will be able to convince people to believe in Allāh. The Prophet ﷺ preached for twenty-three years, and for the first thirteen of those, most people rejected him. They lived with him, saw his miracles, acknowledged his nobility, yet did not believe in his message. Allāh was telling the Prophet ﷺ, and through him, us, that the majority of people will not accept the Truth, no matter how much he desired it. Only a small group embraced the Truth, and most of them were poor, but for Allāh, what matters is the quality, not quantity. The rich and powerful were often the last to join.

---

[100] *at-Tawbah* (9: 128).

وَمَا تَسْـَٔلُهُمْ عَلَيْهِ مِنْ أَجْرٍۚ إِنْ هُوَ إِلَّا ذِكْرٌ لِّلْعَٰلَمِينَ ١٠٤

Even though you are not asking them for a reward for this 'Qur'ān'. It is not except a reminder to the whole world.

Allāh linked this sūrah to the message of our Prophet ﷺ. First, He challenged the Quraysh to reflect on the story of Yūsuf and its source; then He affirmed the sincerity of the Prophet ﷺ towards them. Finally, Allāh told them that the Prophet ﷺ was selfless: ***'...you are not asking them for a reward for this 'Qur'ān'...'*** In this verse, Allāh challenged them to think why one of their own would suffer persecution to preach this message? Why would he go against his nation and preach a doctrine that will only bring him ridicule and hostility? Was he doing it for power, money, or prestige? It is a continuous *Sunnah* of all prophets that they worked tirelessly against all the odds and without remuneration to invite people to Allāh. The *Qur'ān* says that prophets after prophet told their people, 'I am not asking you for any wages, power or reward.'

Allāh forbade for the prophets any worldly reward for their ceaseless work. In the case of the Prophet Muhammad ﷺ, Allāh even disallowed charity, not just for him but also his descendants. All this, so no one doubts the sincerity and selflessness of the messengers.

The Prophet ﷺ lived in poverty, even after the Islamic government in Madīnah became rich and powerful. An incident aptly underscores the Prophet's ﷺ lifestyle. ʿUmar ibn al-Khaṭṭāb said that once he visited the Prophet's ﷺ

private chamber and found him lying on a mat made of a palm tree. Under his head was a leather pillow stuffed with palm fibers, and above him hung a few water skins. On seeing the marks of the mat imprinted on his side, ʿUmar wept. The Prophet ﷺ asked him, 'Why are you weeping?' And ʿUmar replied, 'O Allāh's Messenger ﷺ! Caesar and Khosrau are leading the (luxurious) life while you, Allāh's Messenger ﷺ though you are, are living destitute.' The Prophet ﷺ replied? 'Won't you be satisfied that they enjoy this world and we the Hereafter?[101]

'...It is not except a reminder to the whole world.' *ʿĀlam* is generally translated as 'world' and means every community and group. In one sense, *ʿālam* means the world of human beings, the world of *jinn*, and the world of animals. In another sense, *ʿālam* implies the world of nations: the Romans, Persians, and Chinese, etc. *ʿĀlam* also means a genus or category of people. Allāh said that this Qur'ān is a *dhikr*, or reminder for all people among *jinns* and humans.

In this verse, the Qur'ān is referenced as *Dhikr,* which means remembrance. The Qur'ān has many names: the most common are Qur'ān, *Kitāb*, *Dhikr*, and *Al-Furqān.* The first two names we already discussed at the beginning of this *tafsīr*; and *Al-Furqān* means the criterion that separates good from evil, truth from falsehood and *īmān* from *kufr*. The third most common name of the Qur'ān is *Dhikr*. Calling the Qur'ān a *Dhikr* means that it reminds people of what they already knew. All of us subconsciously

---

[101] *Ṣaḥīḥ* of al-Bukhārī (4913).

know that our Creator and Lord is Allāh, but because of circumstances, some of us forget.

How does humankind already know? Because the Qur'ānic message speaks to the human being's original nature. Allāh ingrained into every one of us the inherent capacity to believe in Him and to want to worship Him. The name for this is *fiṭrah*. It is in our nature to affirm Allāh's existence. Humanity has always acknowledged the presence of a higher power; even the most primitive societies believed in such a being. The Qur'ān uses our *fiṭrah* and intelligence to bring us back to the worship of One God; hence the Qur'ān is called a *Dhikr*.

Dhikr also means a continuous reminder. Another, less known meaning, is that the Qur'ān, being the *Dhikr*, will honour a nation and remind the posterity about them. We find this meaning in Sūrah al-Zukhruf, wherein Allāh says, *'This Qur'ān will be a legacy for you and your people.'*[102] In other words, 'You will have honour because of this Qur'ān.' Before the Qur'ān, the Arabs were considered one of the most backward people of their time. They didn't have a unified government, script, or civilization; the Romans and Persians didn't even see the need to conquer them. Yet barely twenty years after the revelation of the Qur'ān, the Arabs became a unified force under one leader and excelled in knowledge. And within two decades of the founding of an Islamic government in Madinah, they conquered the Persian Empire and carved up the eastern half of the Roman Empire.

[102] *al-Zukhruf* (43: 44).

وَكَأَيِّن مِّنْ ءَايَةٍ فِى ٱلسَّمَٰوَٰتِ وَٱلْأَرْضِ يَمُرُّونَ عَلَيْهَا وَهُمْ
عَنْهَا مُعْرِضُونَ ﴿١٠٥﴾

How many signs in the heavens and the earth do they pass by with indifference?

There are so many signs of Allāh in creation: the sun, the moon, and the stars. There are signs in the oceans, the mountains, and valleys, and there are signs within our souls. There are also human-made signs that we can witness in the remnants of the nations of old, like the dwellings carved into the mountains by the people of ʿĀd and Thamūd (Nabateans). Allāh says, ***'How many signs in the heavens and the earth do they pass by with indifference?'*** Notice the excellent choice of the verb here, *yamurrūn,* meaning to pass by. They are walking by without even thinking. Allāh chooses an exact word. They are turning away from the signs, even as they walk right by them. This is the reality of the state of most of humanity. We see the beautiful signs of Allāh around us, but we don't stop to reflect.

وَمَا يُؤْمِنُ أَكْثَرُهُم بِٱللَّهِ إِلَّا وَهُم مُّشْرِكُونَ ﴿١٠٦﴾

And most of them do not believe in Allāh without associating others with Him 'in worship'.

Another truly profound verse. For the majority of the Quraysh, the problem was not that they didn't believe in Allāh, but rather that they did not ***'...believe in Allāh without associating others with Him.'*** Here, Allāh has highlighted a fundamental point: to believe in Allāh is not the essence of *īmān.* The Quraysh believed in Allāh and that He created them. They believed that Allāh was All-Powerful, but that did not make them Muslims, because they also believed in idols whom they set up as partners with Allāh. Thinking that the false gods had a share in Allāh's power cancelled their claim to belief in Allāh. Allāh, our true Lord, called their polytheistic belief *shirk* as well as a great injustice.

There is also a reminder to Muslims to purify their belief and rid it of *shirk,* whether apparent or hidden. There is a warning in this not to worship wealth, power, and fame. In popular culture, we find people idolizing singers, movie actors, and artists as if they were gods. This verse teaches us that belief in Allāh becomes void by ascribing partners to Him.

أَفَأَمِنُوٓا۟ أَن تَأْتِيَهُمْ غَـٰشِيَةٌ مِّنْ عَذَابِ ٱللَّهِ أَوْ تَأْتِيَهُمُ ٱلسَّاعَةُ
بَغْتَةً وَهُمْ لَا يَشْعُرُونَ ﴿١٠٧﴾

Do they feel secure that an overwhelming torment from Allāh will not overtake them, or that the Hour will not take them by surprise when they least expect 'it'?

Ghāshiyah means something that covers up. Allāh calls His punishment *ghāshiyah* because it covers and overwhelms. Allāh was now threatening the Quraysh. ***'Do they feel secure that an overwhelming torment from Allāh will not overtake them...?'*** He was saying, 'The Signs are clear, the Truth of the Prophet is manifest, and he has shown you so many miracles. Aren't you worried that My punishment might overwhelm you now or on the Day of Judgement?'

Allāh used a rhetorical question at the beginning of this verse: ***'Do they feel secure...?'*** It is an ultimatum, but people often ignore this threatening aspect of the Qur'ān. The Qur'ān appeals through the reward of Paradise and Mercy, but also warns of a frightening punishment. Today, in our attempt to be politically correct, many of us do not want to talk about the Fire of Hell, but the reality is that it exists, and the Qur'ān's threat is not a bluff.

قُلْ هَٰذِهِۦ سَبِيلِىٓ أَدْعُوٓا۟ إِلَى ٱللَّهِ ۚ عَلَىٰ بَصِيرَةٍ أَنَا۠ وَمَنِ
ٱتَّبَعَنِى ۖ وَسُبْحَٰنَ ٱللَّهِ وَمَآ أَنَا۠ مِنَ ٱلْمُشْرِكِينَ ﴿١٠٨﴾

Say, 'O Prophet,' "This is my way. I invite to Allāh with insight, I and those who follow me. Glory be to Allāh, and I am not one of the polytheists."

The Prophet ﷺ was told to say, ***'This is my way. I invite to Allāh...'*** We can see that the path of the Prophet ﷺ leads to Allāh. The Prophet ﷺ is our connection to the

Divine. Notice that Allāh says 'my path' in the singular: *sabīlī*. In Sūrah al-Fātiḥah, we read, 'Guide us on *the* Straight Path.'[103] Therefore, the path to Allāh is one. Our Prophet ﷺ once drew a straight line in the sand and said, 'This is the straight path of Allāh.' Then he drew lines to the right and left, and said, 'These are other paths, and there is no path among them but that a devil is upon it calling to its way.' Then the Prophet ﷺ recited the verse, *'Indeed, this is My Path – perfectly straight. So follow it and do not follow other ways.'*[104] This clearly shows us that the path to Allāh is straight and singular. Whatever goes against the Straight Path, the Qur'ān refers to it in the plural, as in, *'He brings them out from darknesses into the light.'*[105] Truth is one, falsehoods many.

'I invite to Allāh with insight...' The Prophet ﷺ calls to Allāh *'ala baṣīrah*, with an insight that is rooted in the certainty of knowledge. *Baṣīrah* is from *baṣarah*, which means to see. *Baṣīrah* implies a crystal clear view. The Prophet ﷺ said, 'I have left you upon a clear path, its clarity is the same by night or day. No one deviates from it after me but that he will be ruined.'[106] It shows us that we must possess the knowledge to be a faithful follower of the Prophet ﷺ. If we are ignorant, we cannot follow his guidance in the right way.

'...I and those who follow me...' There is a beautiful message here. Whoever claims to be a follower of the Prophet ﷺ must call to the Straight Path according to

[103] *al-Fātiḥah* (1: 6).
[104] *Musnad* of Aḥmad (4423). The verse quoted is Sūrah al-An'ām (6: 153).
[105] *al-Baqarah* (2: 257).
[106] *Sunan* of Ibn Mājah (44).

his methodology. Inviting others to Islam is *farḍ ʿayn*: an obligation for every adult and sane Muslim. One of our biggest problems when it comes to *daʿwah* is our faulty thinking. We think that *daʿwah* is all about intellectual debate and convincing people, but this is a misconception. Calling others to Islam is not only about rational arguments. Throughout the story of Yūsuf, we have seen that the first step in the process of calling people to the Message is perfecting good manners. The number one thing that affects people's hearts is our conduct. Righteous conduct was the primary *daʿwah* of Yūsuf and all prophets, including our own. Therefore every one of us must give *daʿwah* by being a good Muslim in our behavior and manners. This is far more effective than intellectual debate.

'...Glory be to Allāh, and I am not one of the polytheists.' By saying *subḥānAllāh* here, it is as if the Prophet ﷺ was saying, 'And while I am on this path, I am calling to Allāh and praising and glorifying Him. I am never going to be of the polytheists who worship others besides Him.'

وَمَآ أَرْسَلْنَا مِن قَبْلِكَ إِلَّا رِجَالًا نُّوحِىٓ إِلَيْهِم مِّنْ أَهْلِ ٱلْقُرَىٰٓ ۗ
أَفَلَمْ يَسِيرُوا۟ فِى ٱلْأَرْضِ فَيَنظُرُوا۟ كَيْفَ كَانَ عَـٰقِبَةُ ٱلَّذِينَ مِن
قَبْلِهِمْ ۗ وَلَدَارُ ٱلْـَٔاخِرَةِ خَيْرٌ لِّلَّذِينَ ٱتَّقَوْا۟ ۚ أَفَلَا تَعْقِلُونَ ١٠٩

We only sent before you 'O Prophet' men inspired by Us from among the people of the cities. Have the deniers not travelled through the land to see what was the end of those 'destroyed' before them? And surely the 'eternal' Home of the Hereafter is far better for those mindful 'of Allāh'. Will you not then understand?

Allāh reminded the Prophet Muhammad ﷺ that, like him, prophets of the past lived in towns and cities, and suffered at the hands of their people. It is human nature that we find solace in knowing that someone else before us faced similar challenges. Allāh informed the Prophet ﷺ that the nations of other prophets also belied Allāh's message, so don't be overly shocked by the rejection of the Quraysh.

The verse also shows that all the prophets were men, and this is the standard position of Sunnī Islam. There were no female prophets. Some scholars held that Maryam, the mother of ʿĪsā, was a prophetess, but that was not the case. Yes, an angel communicated with her, but she did not receive *waḥy* or a book from Allāh. The fact that the prophets were men does not mean women are spiritually inferior. Men and women are both spiritually equal in the eyes of Allāh. However, both genders have their roles, some of which come from religion and some from culture. Allāh did not consider it appropriate to appoint a woman prophet in any culture.

'Have the deniers not travelled through the land to see what was the end of those 'destroyed' before them?' The Arabs knew the fate of the people of Ṣāliḥ. There were so many other signs of people who perished in the past, so Allāh said, 'Haven't they seen them or considered them?' Every nation and society thinks that it is at its pinnacle and is indestructible. They believe they are the most powerful and have reached the height of civilization. But Allāh is saying, 'You are not the first, and you are not going to be the last to think like that. Stop being so arrogant.'

All of these verses were comforting to our Prophet ﷺ. Allāh was telling him, 'Prophets before you came to people of the past and they, too, had their message rejected. People are blind to the signs in the creation. Your job is only to try your best, but if you are unable to get the results you want, know that ***"...the 'eternal' Home of the Hereafter is far better..."***'

حَتَّىٰٓ إِذَا ٱسْتَيْـَٔسَ ٱلرُّسُلُ وَظَنُّوٓا۟ أَنَّهُمْ قَدْ كُذِبُوا۟ جَآءَهُمْ نَصْرُنَا
فَنُجِّىَ مَن نَّشَآءُ ۖ وَلَا يُرَدُّ بَأْسُنَا عَنِ ٱلْقَوْمِ ٱلْمُجْرِمِينَ ﴿١١٠﴾

And when the messengers despaired and
thought that they were denied (by their
people), Our help came to them 'at last'.
We then saved whoever We willed,
and Our punishment is never averted
from the wicked people.

As mentioned before, there are different recitations of the Qur'ān, and in this verse we have two authentic recitations. Depending on how you recite the verse, the verse reads either '*kudhibū*' or '*kudhdhibū*' (with an emphasis on the middle letter). Both recitations are valid, and each has a different meaning.

'Kudhibū' would translate as, '...and the people thought that the promises of the prophets were false and that they were telling lies'. So Allāh is criticizing these nations for thinking that their prophets were lying to them; when the matter reached this point, they were punished with Divine punishment, and Allāh's safety came to save the people of faith.

'Kudhdhibū' would translate as, '...and the prophets thought that their nations had rejected them'. In this recitation, the prophets came to the realization that their nations would not believe. So there are the two meanings depending on who is the one doing the thinking and doing the assuming. In the first, it's the people who have assumed that the prophets are telling lies. In the second, it's the prophets realizing that the people would not believe. Both of them are correct and true. One of the principles of Qur'ānic recitation is that all Qur'ānic recitations are equally valid.

'...Our help came to them 'at last'. We then saved whoever We willed, and Our punishment is never averted from the wicked people.' Once again, there are two authentic recitations, *nujjiya,* and *nunji,* both complementary in meaning. One of them is in the past tense, and the other in the future. Allāh said that when the time for judgement came, He punished the wrongdoers and saved the messenger. In the other recitation, which is in the future tense, Allāh is informing our Prophet ﷺ that a time will come when Allāh will save him from the wrongdoers, and punish the latter. Our Prophet ﷺ was saved multiple times in the *Sīrah,* including from at least two assassination attempts, and in the battles of Badr, Aḥzāb and Uḥud.

Allāh is saying, 'We saved the people of the past. Surely, We will save you as well.'

لَقَدْ كَانَ فِى قَصَصِهِمْ عِبْرَةٌ لِّأُو۟لِى ٱلْأَلْبَٰبِ ۗ مَا كَانَ حَدِيثًا
يُفْتَرَىٰ وَلَٰكِن تَصْدِيقَ ٱلَّذِى بَيْنَ يَدَيْهِ وَتَفْصِيلَ كُلِّ شَىْءٍ
وَهُدًى وَرَحْمَةً لِّقَوْمٍ يُؤْمِنُونَ ﴿١١١﴾

Indeed, in their stories there was truly a lesson for people of reason. This message cannot be a fabrication, rather 'it is' a confirmation of the previous revelation, a detailed explanation of all things, a guide and a mercy for people of faith.

This verse begins with an emphasis, to bring the point home again and again. ***'Indeed, in their stories, there was truly a lesson for people of reason...'*** *'Ibrah* means lesson and comes from *'abara,* which is to cross over, like crossing over a bridge. *'Ibrah* can also denote wisdom. By reflecting on the stories of the past, one can learn valuable lessons and gain wisdom.

Notice how beautifully this last verse of the sūrah connects with the beginning. Allāh said in the beginning, *'We relate to you 'O Prophet' the best of stories...'*[107] The sūrah started in the present tense and ends in the past tense:

107 *Yūsuf* (12: 3).

'Indeed, in their stories, there was...' Allāh began, 'Indeed, in the story of Yūsuf and his brothers, there are *āyāt* for all *who ask.*'[108] And now He tells us, 'In their stories, there was *'ibrah* for *those of intelligence.*' In the beginning, Allāh said to us that anyone who listens to the story of Yūsuf with an open heart and mind would find miracles and signs. And, now, in the end, Allāh tells us that if we go beyond listening and reflect on the story, we will gain a deeper understanding. We will go beyond the *āyāt* to the *'ibrah,* and there we will discover the hidden wisdom.

'...This message cannot be a fabrication, rather 'it is' a confirmation of previous revelation, a detailed explanation of all things...' When we know that a story is true, psychologically and subconsciously, we hear with a different mind. Allāh is telling us that this isn't a fairy tale: it is a true story and a confirmation of the revelation that came before it.

'...a guide and a mercy for people of faith.' May Allāh make us of the people of *īmān* and faith who are guided by the story of Yūsuf. May He make us among those who follow the footsteps of the Prophet ﷺ in calling people to the path of Allāh. May He make us among those who contemplate this sūrah's message, extract its profound wisdom and benefits, and apply them in our lives. May Allāh help us benefit from the *tawakkul* of Ya'qūb, the patience of Yūsuf, and the *tawbah* of his brothers. And, finally, may Allāh make us the people of the Qur'ān, *āmīn.*

[108] *Yūsuf* (12: 7).

PART THIRTEEN

50 Lessons from Sūrah Yūsuf

50 Lessons from Sūrah Yūsuf

Indeed, in their stories there was truly a lesson for people of reason.

Our reading of the story of Yūsuf is complete. Allāh concludes by reminding us once again that there are many lessons in it. It is as if He is telling us: One reading isn't enough! Read this Sūrah, and then read it again and again, and every time you read, you shall find beneficial lessons and morals. So let us embark on another journey of extracting its lessons. Allāh tells us that in their stories, was ***'...a lesson for the people of reason...'*** Therefore, let's take the time to reflect on the *'ibrah,* the hidden wisdom, and other benefits, this sūrah offers. Below are fifty such lessons.

1. The miracle of the language and eloquence of the Qur'ān

This sūrah shows us the **miracle of the Qur'ān**: its style, recitation, and the intricately interwoven meanings. Everything about the language of the Qur'ān is miraculous, and Sūrah Yūsuf highlights this most profoundly. We are told the story in riveting detail, but without the superfluous events. Contrast this story with its counterparts in other Scriptures and astound yourself at the eloquence of the Qur'ānic version.

2. The stories of the Qur'ān are the best

Allāh said, *"We relate to you 'O Prophet' the best of stories…"*[109] The Qur'ānic stories are the best, and they deserve a close study. We should read them and narrate them to our children, and contemplate deeply on their lessons. Although this *tafsīr* is about Sūrah Yūsuf, let this be a gateway to exploring other stories of the Qur'ān as they all offer amazing insight.

3. When Allāh wants to bless someone, He blesses him with knowledge

Allāh tells us in this sūrah that He had blessed the family of Isḥāq with knowledge, wisdom, and prophethood. The ultimate blessings from Allāh are faith and knowledge. The Prophet ﷺ said, 'If Allāh intends good for someone, He gives to him the understanding of the religion.'[110]

4. The intuition of the believer is true

Of the wisdom of this sūrah is that it shows us that the believer's *firāsah* or intuition is real. *Firāsah* comes from being close to Allāh, and it keeps the believer rightly guided. Ya'qūb's *firāsah* warned him that something was

[109] *Yūsuf* (12: 3).
[110] *Ṣaḥīḥ* al-Bukhārī (71).

wrong concerning Yūsuf. The closer one draws to Allāh, the more accurate their intuition will be. Although it carries no legal weight, the intuition can be used in business or social dealings and making decisions in one's life. *Firāsah* is one of the fruits of piety that Allāh bestows upon the righteous.

5. True dreams and their interpretation are a gift from Allāh

Dreams are a constant motif of Sūrah Yūsuf, beginning with Yūsuf's dream as a child, then the dreams of the prisoners, and finally, that of the King. True dreams and their interpretation are blessings from Allāh, which He bestows upon some of His most righteous servants.

6. The inner beauty of decency and morality is more attractive than outer beauty

The events of the story of Yūsuf show us that inner beauty is the result of one's character. It comes from good manners, chastity, and living a good and wholesome life. No matter how people live their lives, from their *fitrah* or innate nature, they can tell right from wrong. A chaste and virtuous life is a reflection of inner beauty. After Yūsuf refused the sexual advances of the wife of Al-ʿAzīz, she invited her friends to see him. They attested to his outer beauty, but it was his inner beauty, exemplified by his refusal, which made him even more attractive; they thought he was a noble angel. It is human nature to admire an honourable character. Inner beauty increases over time, while outer beauty fades away.

7. Righteousness leads to success in this life and the next

Yūsuf's good character was attested to by all those who knew him: his family, the wife of Al-ʿAzīz, the prisoners, the witnesses, and finally, even the King himself. People testified to the nobility of his character, and the King not only exonerated him of false allegations but also appointed Yūsuf finance minister of Egypt. But Yūsuf's gaze was set on the Hereafter, and he prayed to Allāh to *"Allow me to die as one who submits and join me with the righteous."*[111]

8. The importance of being fair and just

This sūrah teaches us the importance of being fair, just, and equitable with our children, as Ya'qūb was with his. It also tells us that fairness and love are different. A Muslim is required to treat his children fairly, but it is not required of him to love them equally, as he has no control over love. While Yaʿqūb treated all his children justly, he loved Yūsuf and Binyāmīn more, because of which his other sons became jealous and conspired to get rid of Yūsuf.

9. Appreciate the blessings of Allāh and accept what you don't have

Sūrah Yūsuf teaches us to appreciate Allāh's blessings, and be content with what He, out of His wisdom, did not grant us. Sometimes, a thing we covet may turn out to be a bane if it leads us away from the remembrance of Allāh. There is good both in what Allāh gives us and what He withholds from us because He alone knows what is best

[111] *Yūsuf* (12: 101).

for His creation. Imagine if we had even a fraction of the beauty of Yūsuf. Would we have used it honourably?

10. Don't flaunt your blessings

Allāh does not love the boastful. A wise and intelligent believer does not flaunt his blessings because it can displease the bestower of those blessings and may cause jealousy in the hearts of others. When Yaʿqūb learned about Yūsuf's dream and understood its positive implications, he immediately told him not to share it with the brothers lest they hatched a plot out of jealousy.

11. The believer is always cautious

A believer should act cautiously and carefully. When the brothers asked Yaʿqūb's permission to take Binyāmīn, he was reluctant based on his bad experience with their similar request concerning Yūsuf. Our Prophet ﷺ said, 'The believer is not stung twice from the same hole.'[112] The believer should always think through the ramifications of their actions carefully before choosing the course of action.

12. Beautiful patience means not complaining to the people

This sūrah teaches us that patience has different kinds and levels. There is patience during a calamity, in restraining oneself from committing sins, and in persevering in acts worship. The best kind of patience is *ṣabrun jamīl*: beautiful patience. Allāh praised Yaʿqūb for observing *ṣabrun jamīl,* which is that one turns to Allāh during trials, complaining

[112] *Ṣaḥīḥ* of al-Bukhārī (5782).

only to Him about the plight and seeking only His sympathy, and not of the people. The pinnacle of faith is to bear a calamity with patience and fortitude: this is *ṣabrun jamīl*.

13. A good strategy is a part of good faith

This sūrah displays the wisdom of planning. The believer always thinks ten steps ahead. Yūsuf had the plan to put the cup in the sack of his brother, Binyāmīn, so that he could keep him in Egypt. When he started searching the caravan, he began with the older brothers so as not to draw attention to his plan. What it shows us is that the believer is smart, has a good plan, and employs a brilliant strategy.

14. Show respect to your parents in every way possible

Our religion tells us to treat our parents with honour and respect. The actions of Yūsuf demonstrated this. When he welcomed his parents as they arrived in Egypt, he went to the outskirts of the city to greet them, had them sit on the throne, and treated lavishly. For a Muslim, no human being deserves more veneration than his parents.

15. Pious households produce pious children

Allāh mentioned at the beginning of the sūrah that He had completed His favours upon, "*…you and the descendants of Ya'qūb, 'just' as He once perfected it upon your forefathers, Ibrāhīm and Isḥāq.*"[113] These favours sprang from the status Allāh had granted the Prophet Ibrāhīm. In Sūrah al-Kahf, Allāh told us that He had saved the treasure of two orphans because

---

[113] *Yūsuf* (12:6).

their deceased father was a righteous man. The important take away is that if we want our children to be righteous, we have to embody that quality ourselves first.

16. The believers are concerned about their offspring

The believer should always make it a priority to protect their family and children at both the physical and spiritual levels. When Yūsuf told his dream to his father, Ya'qūb immediately wanted to protect him. He didn't boast, 'What a proud father you have made me,' instead, he sought to protect him from potential harm. He wanted the best for Yūsuf in *Dīn* and *Dunya*.

17. Protect your faith and chastity in your youth, and Allāh will protect you in your old age

We learn from Sūrah Yūsuf that if we try to protect our faith and chastity in our youth, Allāh will protect us from corruption in later life. A young man or woman who has a strong relationship with Allāh will rarely lose faith in older age. Yūsuf had *taqwā* of Allāh in his youth, and Allāh preserved it for him in maturity. He resisted temptation during the most vulnerable period of his life–young adulthood–and Allāh honored him in later life. Those who say that they will become pious only when they're old, rarely do.

18. Be on guard against the evils of ego

The story of this sūrah displayed the perils of succumbing to one's ego. Our ego can call us to evil, as the actions of the brothers showed. The wife of Al-'Azīz had suffered from ego, and it harmed her badly. She thought that as a beautiful woman from the elite of Egyptian society, she could coerce a handsome slave to commit an immoral act with her. She was enraged when he refused and avenged him by false accusation and imprisonment. The believers should be more concerned about how Allāh views them, rather than the people.

19. Jealousy is destructive

A critical lesson from Sūrah Yūsuf is that jealousy is one of the most destructive emotions known to humans. It makes an otherwise rational person behave irrationally. In a fit of jealousy, people can do things they never imagined they could. In this story, the brothers of Yūsuf, overcome by acute jealously, tried to do the unthinkable: kill their little brother. Our Prophet ﷺ warned us, 'Beware of envy, for it devours good deeds just as fire devours wood or grass.'[114] That is why we should seek refuge in Allāh from jealousy and try to suppress it as soon as it occurs in our hearts.

20. Dangers of interacting with the opposite gender

Of the lessons we learn from this sūrah one is the dangers of interacting with the opposite gender, especially when it can lead to temptation. Yūsuf and the wife of Al-ʿAzīz were alone together for long periods, and this fuelled her lust. The Prophet ﷺ said, 'Whoever has faith in Allāh and the Last Day, let him not be alone with an unrelated woman without her guardian. Verily, the third of them

---

[114] *Sunan* of Abū Dāwūd (4903).

is *Shayṭān*.'[115] Our religion acknowledges that men and women are naturally attracted to each other, and, for this reason, prescribes avoiding private meetings, lowering of the gaze, and dressing modestly in front of a unrelated person of the opposite gender. We ignore this guidance at our peril.

21. The dangers of unchecked lust

One of the biggest dangers to humanity is unchecked sexual desire and lust. How many people have ruined themselves because of them? Sexual passion can blind a person and lead them to sinful acts, lying, and deceit. The wife of Al-ʿAzīz acted dishonourably because of an overpowering desire. The Prophet ﷺ told us, "There are seven whom Allāh will shade on a day when there is no shade but His," one of whom will be "...a man who is tempted by a beautiful woman of high status but he rejects her, saying, 'I fear Allāh...'"[116]

22. Gossip is an evil trait

The story of Yūsuf teaches us that gossip, slander, and backbiting are evils that distance us from Allāh. The Prophet ﷺ said, 'Part of the perfection of someone's Islam is his leaving alone that which does not concern him.'[117] The believer should not engage in idle talk about others. We saw the evil of gossip in action in this story when the women of the town began gossiping about Yūsuf and the wife of Al-ʿAzīz. Allāh takes this sin so seriously that He

---

115 *Musnad* of Aḥmad (14241).
116 *Ṣaḥīḥ* of al-Bukhārī (629); *Ṣaḥīḥ* of Muslim (1031).
117 *Sunan* of Ibn Mājah (2518).

forbade the gossipmonger from entering *Jannah*. We must defend the honour of a person when people are gossiping about them in their absence.

23. Haste does not bring good

The Prophet ﷺ told us, 'Haste is from *Shayṭān*.'[118] The sūrah taught us not to act hastily. After spending years in prison on false charges, Yūsuf could have rushed out at the first sign of release. But he took time contemplating his next move, and because of this, Yūsuf was able to clear his name, which in turn led to his appointment as the finance minister of Egypt.

24. Desiring a sin is not sin, but acting upon it is

We are not held accountable for passing sinful thoughts, as long as we do not act upon them. We have no control over the evil ideas that *Shayṭān* whispers in our hearts, but our religion has taught us how to protect against them. Allāh explicitly says that Yūsuf *'would have inclined'*[119] towards the wife of Al-ʿAzīz, but his fear of Allāh prevented him from acting on that desire. To control an unlawful urge is the essence of *taqwā*.

25. The only way to control a sinful urge is to turn to Allāh

Sūrah Yūsuf illustrated that the most effective way to control a sinful urge is to turn to Allāh. In the scene of the women at the banquet, when they tried to tempt Yūsuf,

---

118 *Sunan* al-Tirmidhī (2012).

119 *Yūsuf* (12: 24).

he turned to Allāh and made a sincere supplication. Those who remain steadfast in the face of temptation will taste the sweetness of faith.

26. The fruits of patience are always sweet

The story of Yūsuf showed us the sweetness of patience. With patience, Yūsuf rose to a lofty position, Ya'qūb reunited with Yūsuf, and the bothers repented for their wrong actions. For years, Yūsuf patiently waited in the dungeon, only to see his patience land him in the court of the King. Our beloved Prophet ﷺ remained patient in adversity, and Allāh raised him to the highest station. Allāh assures us that He is definitely with *as-sābirīn*. The prophets endured prolonged persecutions patiently, but then Allāh said, *"Our help came to them 'at last'."*[120] For patience, Allāh promises *bi ghayri hisāb:* reward without measure.

27. A believer should not hurt the feelings of others

A wisdom that we learn from this sūrah is not to hurt others' feelings. Yūsuf's conduct throughout the story exemplified this characteristic. Despite the enormity of the brothers' crime against him, Yūsuf concealed their faults and spared them the embarrassment. He didn't even ask them why they threw him in the well, and when they admitted their guilt, he said, *"No blame will there be upon you today."*[121] How many among us can come close to the graciousness of Yūsuf?

---

[120] *Yūsuf* (12: 110).
[121] *Yūsuf* (12: 92).

28. Generosity influences hearts and minds

Muslims throughout the world are famous for generosity towards their guests, and Sūrah Yūsuf showed its highest manifestation. Our Prophet ﷺ said, 'Whoever believes in Allāh and the Last Day, let him honour his guest.'[122] After the brothers first came to Yūsuf, he gave them a generous amount of grains, and even returned their capital, saying, *"Do not you see that I give full measure and I am the best of hosts?"*[123] He opened their hearts and minds by showing his generosity.

29. When preaching Islam, our actions should speak louder than our words

Sūrah Yūsuf showed us that we should practice what we preach. When calling people to Islam, we should be the embodiment of our faith, as Yūsuf was when he spoke to his fellow prisoners. Many of us mistakenly think that all we have to do is tell others about our religion, without practicing it ourselves. Throughout this sūrah, we see that Yūsuf established his moral character, honesty, integrity, tenderness, and *iḥsān* before preaching. When the fellow prisoners saw Yūsuf's virtues, they said to him? *"...we surely see you as one of the good-doers."*[124] Once this was established, and the opportunity presented itself, Yūsuf preached them about Islam.

---

[122] *Ṣaḥīḥ* of al-Bukhārī (5672).
[123] *Yūsuf* (12: 59).
[124] *Yūsuf* (12: 36).

30. Daʿwah requires the right setting and a willing audience

This sūrah teaches us that a caller to Islam should wait for the right time and place to convey the message. When the two prisoners came to Yūsuf with their questions, he said, *"No food will come to you as your provision, but I will have informed you of its interpretation before it comes."*[125] He prepared them mentally for listening to his *daʿwah.*

31. When calling to Islam, we should begin with *Tawḥīd*

Yūsuf's *daʿwah to the prisoners* combined the three types of *tawḥīd* and the pillars of our religion. What sets Islam apart from other religions is the simplicity of our creed. Yūsuf's call to Islam highlighted this most succinctly and convincingly. Our faith calls for belief in One Allāh, the prophets, and the Judgement Day.

32. *Tawakkul* and the necessity of using the means to reach the goal

Sūrah Yūsuf reinforces the right concept of *tawakkul* or the reliance on Allāh. *Tawakkul* means that we do whatever is needed or possible while relying on Allāh. By asking the freed prisoner to mention him to the King, Yūsuf used the means available to him. Both the goal and the road that leads to it are from Allāh. Some Muslims erroneously think that trusting Allāh means sitting back and doing nothing. True *tawakkul* is to do our level best to achieve

---

[125] *Yūsuf* (12: 37).

our goal, all the while believing that the results are in the hands of Allāh.

33. Civic engagement in society is a part of Islam

Some Muslims say that it is *ḥarām* to participate in the civic or governmental institutions of a non-Muslim society. Yet in this sūrah, we see that Yūsuf asked to become a minister to a non-Muslim King. Allāh said, *"He could not have taken his brother under the King's law, but Allāh had so willed."*[126] Yūsuf obeyed the law of the land, and Allāh made a way out for him. What we learn from this is that we should fight for our rights in the court system, as long as what we are seeking is Islamically permissible. Our faith encourages us to participate in projects that help society. We should, of course, not involve in anything that would violate the tenets of our faith.

34. Islam allows secondary evidence to determine the truth

This sūrah teaches us that it is permissible to use secondary evidence to establish the truth. When the sons told Yaʿqūb that a wolf had killed Yūsuf, from the bloodied but untorn shirt he realized Yūsuf was alive. When Al-ʿAzīz's wife ran after Yūsuf and tore his shirt from the back, it proved his innocence. In each case, the shirt provided the secondary evidence. In our *Sharīʿah*, it is allowed to use secondary evidence and take into account external factors, even if there were no two witnesses to the crime.

---

[126] *Yūsuf* (12: 76).

35. Injustice is part of worldly life; true justice is for the Hereafter

We see Yūsuf enduring many injustices with patience. A believer should know that there is no avoiding injustice in this imperfect world. This does not mean we should accept injustice, but instead we should fight it with all legal means. Should we fail to get justice in this world, we must believe that every wronged person will get their rights in the court of Allāh in the Hereafter.

36. The believer always ascribes good to Allāh and evil to *Shayṭān*

One of the lessons we learn from the actions of Yaʿqūb and Yūsuf in this sūrah is that the true believer always ascribes good to Allāh and evil to *Shayṭān*. Yūsuf said in the concluding passages of the story, *"He was truly kind to me when He freed me from prison and brought you all from the desert after Shayṭān had ignited rivalry between my siblings and me..."*[127] He ascribed the blessings to Allāh and blamed *Shayṭān* for causing problems. This is the way a believer should understand good and evil.

37. *Shayṭān* is ever eager to cause problems between Muslims, especially family members

Much of this story is about the plots of *Shayṭān* and his role in fomenting jealousy and temptation. We see that he is keen to cause problems between the believers, especially between family members. *Shayṭān* caused the

---

[127] *Yūsuf* (12: 100).

brothers to be jealous of Yūsuf, so much so, that they even intended to kill him. Behind many of the family problems, we can find the hand of *Shayṭān*. When disputes arise in the family, we should pause and think about how *Shayṭān* might be instigating the issue and seek protection from Allāh.

38. You won't succeed without experiencing failure

One of the lessons of the sūrah is that we will not succeed until we have failed. Yūsuf was born into the household of a prophet, yet he ended up dumped in a well, sold into slavery, falsely accused of seduction, and thrown into jail. But after patient perseverance, he found himself sitting on a minister's chair in the palace of the King of Egypt. The entire story is a cycle of ups and downs, and our lives are like that. We won't succeed until we have shown Allāh that we can deal with failure.

39. Complaining to Allāh is a part of *īmān*

One crucial lesson this sūrah teaches is that complaining to Allāh is a sign of *īmān*. When Yaʿqūb heard about Binyāmīn's enslavement in Egypt, he said, *"I complain of my anguish and sorrow only to Allāh"*[128] He did so to elicit Allāh's sympathy and mercy. He didn't do it to question Allāh's decision, but to invoke His mercy. On the other hand, when we complain to the people about our tough situation, that is not a sign of strong *īmān*.

---

[128] *Yūsuf* (12: 86).

40. The best therapy is *duʿā'*

Supplicating to Allāh in times of distress is therapeutic. When grief strikes, the righteous turn to Allāh for comfort. When they feel powerless and overwhelmed, it's Allāh they turn to for their needs. When Yūsuf faced the temptation of seduction, he sincerely turned to Allāh, *"My Lord! I would rather be in jail than do what they invite me to. And if You do not turn their cunning away from me, I might yield to them and fall into ignorance."*[129] The believer calls out to Allāh to help them deal with fear, grief, and temptations.

41. Genuine repentance requires regret and remorse

Sinning intentionally and hoping that Allāh will forgive, is not repentance. Before they committed the crime, the brothers of Yūsuf said, *"Kill Yūsuf or cast him out to some 'distant' land then after that, you may 'repent, and' become righteous people!"*[130] They thought, 'We'll do the crime, and Allāh will forgive us, and everything will be fine after that.' That type of repentance is not accepted. Their repentance was only accepted at the end of the sūrah when they genuinely asked Yūsuf and their father to forgive them for their crimes. True repentance also means resolving in the heart never to return to that sin. Allāh does not look at the quantity of our sins; He looks at the quality of our repentance.

---

[129] *Yūsuf* (12: 33).
[130] *Yūsuf* (12: 9).

42. If you have wronged someone, you should ask for their forgiveness

The general rule is that one's sins are between them and Allāh. But if someone sinned against a person, they need to apologize to that person. The brothers had committed a crime against their father and Yūsuf, and, therefore, they apologized to both. Following their apology, they also repented to Allāh.

43. Forgive, especially within family and when you are in power

Real forgiveness is when someone forgives at the height of power. Yūsuf forgave the brothers when he could have exacted revenge, and he did so humbly. He said, *"There is no blame on you today. May Allāh forgive you! He is the Most Merciful of the merciful!"*[131] Our Prophet ﷺ repeated these words, standing at the doors of the Kaʿbah after the Conquest of Makkah. Neither of them brought up things that had happened in the past. Forgiving is always virtuous, and this is especially so within one's own family.

44. Be careful with what you say to those you don't trust

This sūrah also teaches us that giving an excuse to someone untrustworthy can have unintended consequences. Be careful what you say to those with an evil disposition: it might come back to harm you. This was the case when

[131] *Yūsuf* (12: 92).

Ya'qūb inadvertently told the brothers that he feared that while they were busy racing, a wolf would eat Yūsuf. They used the exact excuse for the disappearance of Yūsuf.

45. Allāh can reconcile the worst enemies and the most hated of siblings and relatives

The example of Yūsuf and his brothers shows us that Allāh can bring about reconciliation between two people, no matter how serious their enmity. Allāh guided Yūsuf to forgive and forget his brothers' crime and guided them to repent sincerely.

46. When confronting a criminal, raise his crime against Allāh first

The events of this sūrah show us that we should always advise the criminal to fear Allāh first, and then our grievance. The first thing Ya'qūb said was, *"Your souls must have tempted you to do something 'evil'..."*[132] He reminded them that they had committed an offense against Allāh. Unfortunately, we often only worry about the rights of the victims and forget that violation of Allāh's rights should be of greater concern.

47. All people have some good in them, so don't give up hope of good from sinners!

Even the worst sinner can eventually repent and change their ways as this sūrah shows. The brothers went from

[132] *Yūsuf* (12: 18).

would-be murderers to sincere repenters and eventually prophets.

48. Turning to Allāh will help us overcome our desires

When you need help to overcome the passions of your soul, body, or the diseases of the heart – turn to Allāh. In his suffering, Yūsuf turned to Allāh, *"So his Lord responded to him, turning their cunning away from him. Surely He is the All-Hearing, All-Knowing."*[133] What this shows is that there is no disease, passion, lust, or desire plaguing our heart from which Allāh cannot save us. We just have to beseech His help.

49. Allāh saves the righteous in the most hopeless situation

All of Yūsuf's situations had seemed hopeless, but Allāh delivered him from every one of them, and He called his story the best story that Muslims will continue to recite until the end of time. But this happened because even in the darkest hours, Yūsuf always called upon Allāh to rescue him.

50. On life's journey, what matters is where we ended, not where we began

One of the great lessons we learn from Sūrah Yūsuf is that Allāh decides our fate according to our last actions, not first. Our condition at the time of our death will dictate our

---

[133] *Yūsuf* (12: 34).

place in the Hereafter. By doing this, Allāh throws a lifeline to the sinners–no matter what your sins, you have yet another chance to return to your Lord in true repentance. It is never too late to give up a lifestyle of evil and replace it with one of righteousness. The example of the brothers of Yūsuf demonstrates this for us. That is why Yūsuf's *duʿā'* at the end of this story is so powerful: O Allāh, *"Allow me to die as one who submits and join me with the righteous."*[134]

[134] *Yūsuf* (12: 101).

Conclusion

The Ring Composition Theory of Sūrah Yūsuf

Some modern researchers[135] have pointed out a remarkable symmetry with regards to this sūrah; the themes in it are like concentric rings, working inwards, climaxing at a middle point (in this case, the dream of the King), and then working outwards in the same order. It can be described as a ring where a letter contrasts with its opposite (**A** with **A'**), and the numbers indicate the verses of the sūrah: (see diagram next page)

[135] See: Jawad Anwar Qureshi, "Ring Composition In Sūrah Yūsuf," *JIQSA*, vol. 2 (2017), pp. 149–168. I have modified slighty from the version of the author.

A 1–3 Preface
B 4–6 Yūsuf's Dream
C 7–18 Yūsuf and his brothers: separated from Ya'qūb
D 19–22 Yūsuf is a slave in Egypt
E 23–24 Yūsuf resists the wife of the Minister out of loyalty
F 24–29 Yūsuf is tempted by the wife of the Minister
G 30–32 Yūsuf is displayed in front of the ladies of the nobility who cut their hands
H 33–35 Yūsuf is imprisoned
I 36–41 Yūsuf interprets dreams for the prisoners
J 42 The freed prisoner forgets Yūsuf
K 43–44 The dream of the King
J' 45 The freed prisoner remembers Yūsuf
I' 46–49 Yūsuf interprets the dream of the King
H' 50 Yūsuf is released from prison
G' 51 The ladies of the nobility testify to his innocence
F' 51 Yūsuf is exonerated by the wife of the Minister
E' 52–53 Yūsuf is exonerated in front of the Ministers
D' 54–57 Yūsuf is made the keeper of the storehouses
C' 58–98 Yūsuf and his brothers are reunited with Ya'qūb
B' 99–101 Fulfillment of Yūsuf's dream
A' 102–111 Conclusion

So if one were to take any section – say, for example, F, it is remarkable to note that as the story proceeds and works its way to the dream of the King, it then begins to work its way back *in the exact same order*. Therefore just as the sixth aspect of the story (in our case, represented by the letter F) deals with Yūsuf being tempted by the wife of the

Minister, the sixth-to-last point (in our case, F') shows Yūsuf being exonerated by the wife of the Minister. This is in its mirror opposite order and demonstrates perfect symmetry. The same applies to all other points of the story. This is an indication of the supreme eloquence of the Qur'ān and yet another mechanism of demonstrating its Divine Origin.

As we conclude this work, it is vital to remember that what our faith requires from us isn't just the *memorization* of knowledge but rather its *implementation* in our lives. Let us read these lessons and absorb their morals not merely to wonder at the beauty of this ever-fascinating saga of real life, but to imbibe them and manifest them in our daily routines and our journey through the trials and tribulations of our own lives.

We know this is the best of all stories, and we are told that in these stories are lessons for people who ponder and reflect. May this work be the beginning of a life-long reflection and implementation, not just of this sūrah, but of the entire Qur'ān! Ameen.

Index